Canning & Preserving
with Ashley English

HOMEMADE
LIVING

Canning & Preserving

with Ashley English

All You Need to Know to Make Jams, Jellies, Pickles, Chutneys & More

LARK
BOOKS
A Division of Sterling Publishing Co., Inc.
New York / London

Senior Editor: Nicole McConville

Editor: Linda Kopp

Editorial Assistant: Beth Sweet

Creative Director: Chris Bryant

Layout & Design: Eric Stevens

Illustrator: Eric Stevens

Photographer: Lynne Harty

Cover Designer: Eric Stevens

This book is FSC Chain-of-Custody certified and has been printed and bound in a responsible manner using recycled materials and agri-based inks.

FSC

Mixed Sources
Product group from well-managed forests, controlled sources and recycled wood or fiber

Cert no. SW-COC-000952
www.fsc.org
© 1996 Forest Stewardship Council

Library of Congress Cataloging-in-Publication Data

English, Ashley, 1976-
  Homemade living : canning & preserving with Ashley English : all you need to know to make ja
jellies, pickles, chutneys & more. -- 1st ed.
    p. cm.
  Includes bibliographical references and index.
  ISBN 978-1-60059-491-5 (HC-PLC : alk. paper)
  1. Canning and preserving. I. Title.
  TX603.E54 2010
  641.4'2--dc22

                  2009024457

10 9 8 7 6 5 4 3 2 1

First Edition

Published by Lark Books, A Division of
Sterling Publishing Co., Inc.
387 Park Avenue South, New York, NY 10016

Text © 2010, Ashley English
Photography © 2010, Lark Books, a Division of Sterling Publishing Co., Inc., unless otherwise spec
Illustrations © 2010, Lark Books, a Division of Sterling Publishing Co., Inc., unless otherwise speci

Distributed in Canada by Sterling Publishing,
c/o Canadian Manda Group, 165 Dufferin Street
Toronto, Ontario, Canada M6K 3H6

Distributed in the United Kingdom by GMC Distribution Services,
Castle Place, 166 High Street, Lewes, East Sussex, England BN7 1XU

Distributed in Australia by Capricorn Link (Australia) Pty Ltd.,
P.O. Box 704, Windsor, NSW 2756 Australia

If you have questions or comments about this book, please contact:
Lark Books
67 Broadway
Asheville, NC 28801
828-253-0467

Manufactured in Canada

ISBN 13: 978-1-60059-491-5

For information about custom editions, special sales, premium and corporate purchases, please
contact Sterling Special Sales Department at 800-805-5489 or specialsales@sterlingpub.com.

For information about desk and examination copies available to college and university
professors, requests must be submitted to academic@larkbooks.com. Our complete policy
can be found at www.larkbooks.com.

Table of Contents

Introduction

A movement is building, in city apartments and country kitchens, as more and more of us reconsider how food ends up on our plates. Chances are if you're reading this book, then you're already on board with—or at least intrigued and inspired by—the local foods movement. It may be that an intention to eat more local foods has prompted you to learn what's involved in making your own jams and pickles.

Home canning is one of the easiest ways to move a bit closer to your food. If you've got a stovetop, a big pot, some jars and lids, and access to fresh produce, then you're all set to get boiling. Home canning can be as elaborate or as simple as you'd like it to be. It doesn't matter if you have a pressure canner or simply a stockpot, a world of possibilities are available to make the harvest last. Whether your intention is to make pickles with the cucumbers running rampant in your garden or to turn those peaches you scored at the farmers' market into delicious jam, home canning and preserving is the way to go.

My own introduction to the alchemy of home canning came at a very young age. Ruby (aka "Nanny"), my maternal grandmother, seemed to spend most of her summer days boiling, stirring, pouring, and pickling something. I can recall with absolute clarity the clanging lid of her canner, the burgundy jars filled with just-pressed grape juice, and the shelves of her garage lined with home-canned corn, green beans, and bread-and-butter pickles. While it would be years before I got around to "taking up the jar" myself, Nanny's garage full of homemade provisions hung around the edges of my culinary memory, nudging gently from the sidelines. It whispered quietly to me each October, encouraging me to make applesauce every time I looked at my mom's apple tree, its branches a positively scandalous display of abundant fruit. It urged, "You can *do* this," whenever I strolled past farmers' market tables burdened under mountains of cucumbers and tomatoes.

Making homemade preserves couldn't be easier. In fact, I'd be willing to wager that once you get started, you'll wonder why it took you so long to discover the inherent joy (not to mention tastiness!) of "putting by." Maybe you're searching for a way to prolong that just-picked flavor of ripe tomatoes, making it available for enjoyment year-round. Perhaps you'd like to make your own baby food, doing so both economically and secure in the knowledge that your child is eating the freshest, safest, most nutritious fruits and vegetables available. Or maybe you're even interested in starting up a small production jam-making business. Whatever brings you to home canning, be assured that the journey is just as rewarding as the destination.

In this book you'll find clear information to help you get started, how-to steps, invaluable troubleshooting tips, plus tons of inspiration. I've provided a primer on the chemistry of canning, so you know what you're doing is safe, along with detailed descriptions of what to look for when selecting ingredients. You'll find ideas for dressing up your jars for gift giving, along with suggestions for canning parties. Why not whip up some fig jam and hang with your best pals (or make new ones) at the same time? There are also recipes, from tried-and-true canning classics to modern twists that might become your new favorites. Each one is offered according to seasonal availability, created and consumed with delight in my very own kitchen.

My sincerest desire is that this book provides you with just the right amount of instruction, creative challenge, and comfort to get you started on your own canning adventures. The information offered here will help you avoid some of the pitfalls encountered by those who "put a lid on things" long ago. You'll make some messes (berry-stained fingers among them), you'll craft some masterpieces, and you'll find the simple joy that comes from making magic in your kitchen.

Ashley English

ABOUT THE AUTHOR

Two years ago, I was hopping in my car each morning, heading off to a job in a medical office. Things changed, though, when a whirlwind romance quickly resulted in marriage, a little homestead at the end of a dirt road, and just the encouragement and support I needed to make some serious life changes. Combining my long-standing interest and education in nutrition, sustainability, and local food, I made the bold decision to leave my stable office job and try my hand at homesteading. It was a huge leap of faith, but I truly believed there was opportunity waiting in a simpler, pared-down life. My goal was to find ways to nourish both body and soul through mindful food practices. And so I jumped in, rubber boots first, completely unaware of what lay ahead.

In my desire to chronicle the triumphs and also the lessons of crafting a homemade life, I started up a blog, Small Measure (www.small-measure. blogspot.com). In it, I try to convey the same ideals I live every day: there are small, simple measures you can take to enhance your life while also caring for your family, community, and the larger world. It's been a trial-and-error experiment in living, encountering setbacks along with the joy. I've learned so much along the way, and I hope this book serves as continual encouragement for you, whether you want to try a little kitchen canning or are contemplating a more major leap of your own.

Chapter 1

Why We Can

Capturing the heady sweetness of ripe peach
bottling up the juiciness of sun-ripened tomatoes, transforming crisp apples into spicy,
buttery spreads—all acts of food alchemy ma
possible to you through canning and preserving. By putting up the best of the season's fla
vors when they are at their peak, you can rev
in a parade of culinary delights all year round
Imagine the pleasure of savoring fragrant che
ry marmalade on crispy toast when snow is
falling outside, or devouring pickled asparagu
alongside a smoky Gouda during an autumn
picnic. While sublime flavor is the ultimate go
in any form of cooking, in the case of canning
safety must also be considered paramount.
Here we'll take a quick peek at the origins of
home canning and how that history has led u
to where home canning is today.

TIME IN A BOTTLE

Consuming preserved foods and beverages has never been as easy as it is today. Pad into the kitchen in your slippers, open the fridge, drink orange juice straight from the carton, and your thirst is quenched, the beverage remains at a hospitable temperature to prevent spoilage, life is good. Before bottling and canning methods were invented, let alone refrigeration, food preservation was achieved through drying, salting, smoking, and pickling in vinegar. Those methods preserved well, but could only be applied to certain types of foods.

Who'd have guessed Napoleon Bonaparte would have so much to do with culinary history? The prolonged and far-reaching Napoleonic Wars prompted the need for a new means of extending the shelf life of foods. The Little Corporal once famously stated "an army marches on its stomach." In order for those stomachs to be satiated and battle-ready, they needed nonperishable, easily transported foods. At the end of the 18th century, Bonaparte's government placed an ad in the French newspaper *Le Monde* offering 12,000 francs to anyone able to invent a new means of preserving food for his army and navy. The stipulation was that the end product must be inexpensive to manufacture in large quantities, easy to transport, and offer soldiers a more nutritious meal than their current ration of salted meat and hardtack. The MREs (Meal, Ready to Eat) of modern armies wouldn't make their appearance on the military meal scene for some time to come.

Enter French confectioner and chef Nicolas Appert. After initially beginning his career experimenting with preserving fruits,

he later concentrated his work on bettering preserving methods for all types of foods. Borrowing from and building on the experimentation of chefs and chemists preceding him, Appert devised the wide-mouthed glass-bottle water bath method of preserving that underlies home canning as it exists today. Reports on the success of the French navy's experiment with his canned goods gained the attention of the French government, ultimately securing him the cash prize on the condition that he put down in words a detailed description of his methods. After the publication of Appert's book in 1810, a timely and, some argue, cunning London entrepreneur named Peter Durand purchased a patent in England for preserving foods, the means of which were strikingly similar to Appert's. He did make a number of alterations and substitutions to Appert's method, however, like also allowing the use of pottery and tinned iron canisters, later shortened colloquially to "cans."

Several decades later, after tin cans were in widespread use in America, an inventor and metalsmith from New York named John L. Mason upped the home-preservation ante by developing the appropriately titled glass "mason" jar. What distinguished Mason's jar from those previously used in home canning was a threaded top, to which a zinc lid with a rubber ring was screwed on. It was the rubber surrounding the lid that created a vacuum seal, protecting food from spoilage. Until Mason's invention, home canners used a flat tin lid topped with sealing wax. Thanks to the ease of use and low cost of Mason's jars, the practice of home canning opened to a wide audience, from city slickers to country folk. By the end of the 19th century, as the cost of cane sugar fell and the development of wood stoves made the process of cooking less physically cumbersome, mason jars were put to increasingly greater use. Summer gardens were planted to produce abundant yields, the surplus of which was "put up" for winter consumption. The Ball family began purchasing small glass bottle makers,

Vintage jars, while not suitable for use now, make an attractive collection.

eventually becoming the largest manufacturer of mason jars in the United States. The new technology, coupled with widespread manufacture, brought home canning into every kitchen.

WAR AND PEAS

Then along came grocery stores. The year 1916 brought the first "cash and carry" food store. For the first time ever, shoppers were permitted to peruse store shelves at their leisure, selecting from a wide variety of items. When large-scale grocery stores opened their doors, the way people interact with their food was forever changed. "You mean there's more than one brand of canned corn out there?" The advent of the grocery store marked a reduction in the number of home canners. Housewives of the time questioned the merits of home canning, and understandably so, when so many convenience foods were now available for purchase.

Home canning resurfaced during both world wars (see "The Taste of Victory"), only to then retreat from public view for several decades. It appeared again among back-to-basics advocates in the 1960s and 1970s. Truthfully, though, it never really disappeared. Homemakers have been making relishes and putting up preserves for as long as home processing has been possible. There is an inherent logic found in preserving your own foods, I'd argue. I'm not alone in this attitude either. For a growing number, the questionable nutritional quality and safety of many packaged foods, coupled with an increasing awareness about the distances foods are shipped to reach consumers, have kindled a desire to take up home canning and preserving. Some gather up their ingredients fresh from their own backyard gardens, while others visit nearby orchards, farmers' markets, and grocers for seasonally available, local foods.

The Taste of Victory

World War I brought changes in attitude toward both growing food and preserving it. Many national governments began encouraging citizens to plant Victory Gardens, also referred to as "Liberty" and "War" gardens. These gardens allowed commercially produced food, and the materials used to make them, to be reallocated for military purposes. The Victory Garden movement was huge, reaching across North America and Europe. Home canning became essential again. Gardening and canning became symbols far surpassing their obvious use in providing sustenance to families. They came to be regarded as a civic obligation, a gesture of nationalistic pride and support. "Of Course I Can" was a popular poster of the day. A self-sufficient citizenry freed up its government to devote attention and resources to winning the battles abroad, or so went the general thinking of the time.

The same mentality and efforts resurfaced during World War II, with Victory Gardens again adorning backyards, rooftops, appropriated vacant lots, and even the White House lawn, courtesy of Eleanor Roosevelt. Redefining the role of what a first lady does, and hoping to set an example and spark participation in gardening, in 1943 she had a portion of the White House lawn dug up for a vegetable garden. The legacy of her action was enormous, with over 20 million Americans following her lead and tilling the soil of their own yards and community gardens. It's estimated that by the end of the war, over 40 percent of produce in the United States was being grown on these small plots. First Lady Michelle Obama, borrowing inspiration from Roosevelt, hopes to inspire a new generation of home gardeners with the revival of the White House garden.

Locavore

A locavore is a person who eats food grown or produced within a certain radius from where they live, usually 50, 100, or 150 miles. Proponents of locavorism believe that local, seasonally available foods are more nutritious, better-tasting, and exact less of an environmental toll than those grown in far-flung locations and then shipped great distances until they reach their designated market. Additionally, locavores advocate eating locally to assist in allowing food economies to remain small in scale and, as a result, more self-sufficient.

Food Miles

Interest in eating locally is intrinsically linked to the concept of food miles, which refers to the distance a given food item travels before it reaches its ultimate consumer. Another way of phrasing this would be to consider a food's distance "from farm to table." Food miles are a key factor in appraising the environmental impact of any food, assessing the amount of nonrenewable resources utilized in transit. It is not uncommon for many foods to travel anywhere between 1500 and 2500 miles (2400 and 4000 km) until they reach consumers. The concept and consideration of food miles is part of the broader movement of sustainability. Many people are turning to farmers' markets or growing their own foods when possible to curtail the fossil fuels consumed to fuel their diet.

Portrait of a Canner

Libby

Summer's activities are pretty much summed up in one word for Libby: canning. From June to September, this fiber artist can be found in her kitchen, stirring, boiling, lifting, wiping, and jarring ample quantities of peaches, pears, pickles of every persuasion imaginable, tomatoes, pasta sauces, beans, soup bases, jellies, and jams, among other things. While she also freezes some of the bounty of produce from her garden, she finds that canned foods are more convenient, requiring no defrost time before they can be put to use.

Libby, like many home canners, learned the technique from her mother and grandmother. While no legitimate claims can be made linking home canning with longevity, her grandmother, who canned and gardened fastidiously for years, lived to the age of 102! Libby has since taught her daughter how to can. Her motivation for incorporating the trade into her own culinary skill set, as well as sharing the wisdom with her family, stems from a desire to get a bit closer to the origins of her food. "I know where it came from and how it was raised and preserved. That provides much comfort and pleasure." She's been at it for over 35 years, so clearly the rewards reaped far transcend the sweaty brows incurred by her summertime labor of love.

Chapter 2
Tools of the Trade

Much of the equipment needed in order to proper can at home is most likely already in your kitchen Investing in a few specialized items will make the process both easier and safer. The good news is that home canning needn't break the bank. Many people opt to start canning in the first place because of the long-term savings incurred by doing so. Take a look around your kitchen and determin what you already have and what might be missin If you lack an item, consider asking around before you buy new. Chances are, you'll find a neighbor, relative, or fellow canner in your community who would gladly loan, barter, or sell the necessary ite to you. Used goods and thrift stores can also be a reservoir of gently worn kitchen items yearning for a second chance. Yard and estate sales are als worth checking out for canning treasure.

CANNING JARS

Come summertime, you can find canning jars in just about every grocery store. Many hardware stores will also have packages of them on hand. The only type of jar that I recommend for canning is the mason-style jar with a threaded top. Mason jars are made of tempered glass and are able to withstand the high temperatures that are reached in both boiling water baths and pressure canning. Best of all, they can be used again and again. Each time you get ready to put up a batch of something, inspect your jars to ensure that they have no cracks, breaks, or chips and are safe to use. Otherwise, you might find yourself dealing with a canner full of leaked pickles or jam or a lid that fails to seal.

Mason jars are available in a variety of sizes, from 4 ounces to quarts (120 mL to 1 L). Gallons (3.8 L) are also available, but they are bulky and cumbersome and, because of their size, need a long processing time to ensure that all microorganisms packed in the center have been destroyed. As such, they are suggested only for processing highly acidic juices, such as grape juice. If you're into appearances, like me, and want a range of looks, rest assured that there is a canning jar out there to suit any style, from traditional to modern. Square jars with platinum-colored lids, my personal favorite, are now available in several sizes. Although I love the look of European jars with rubber gaskets and clamps, I cannot in good conscience recommend them here, as they are not considered safe by all federal food agencies.

So, how do you know which size to use? While most recipes will tell you how many pints or half-pints a recipe will make, consider the quantity of the preserved food that your family is likely to quickly consume, and select your jar size accordingly. If you are a household of one, stick with half-pints. Larger families may wish to use larger jars. Mason jars are available with either wide or tapered mouths. Wide-mouthed jars are suggested if you will be packing large items such as whole tomatoes, dill pickles, or peach halves, as they are easier to both fill and to empty.

Although you might be tempted to repurpose mayonnaise, applesauce, or pickle jars from commercially produced foods, I would suggest you resist the urge. Such jars are made for a single use and may crack or break when up against the temperatures used in home canning. It would be a real shame to spend hours preparing apples and

Canning jars come in a variety of sizes and shapes.

cooking them down to a lovely applesauce, only to be left with a sloppy mess inside your canner from a cracked jar. Instead, repurpose such jars in your pantry, where you can use them to safely store grains, legumes, and baking items. Similarly, antique canning jars, while fabulous for holding cotton balls and swabs in the bathroom, ought not be used for modern home canning. These jars may not be tempered properly or have minute flaws in them, making them susceptible to breakage during processing.

Assorted lids and screw bands

A stainless-steel stockpot

CANNING LIDS AND SCREW BANDS

Modern home canning closures are comprised of a two-piece lid and screw band. The flat lids are fashioned from tin-plated steel that has been covered in a food-grade coating. Running the circumference of the underside of the lid is a rubber compound, specially formulated for vacuum-sealing foods canned at home. After processing, the vacuum seal produces a permanent impression in the lid, thereby rendering it unsafe for reuse. Once you've used a lid, it cannot be used in canning again. It doesn't have to go into the trash can, however. Use the jar for storing dry goods in your pantry, or save up lids and give them to a local elementary school for arts and crafts projects. (I remember making canning-lid Christmas ornaments!)

The lid doesn't go it alone, but completes its task with the aid of its trusty partner, the screw band. This threaded metal band fits atop the lid, securing it in place over the neck of the glass jar. During processing, the screw band holds down the lid, allowing the sealing compound to work its magic and secure the lid to the jar. Once the jar has been processed and allowed to cool, the screw band may be removed. In fact, it should be, at least temporarily. Moisture

may be present under the screw band and, if not removed and dried, rust may occur, prohibiting reuse of the band for future processing. If cared for properly, screw bands may be used multiple times. Once they show signs of wear, such as warping or rusting, it's time to safely discard or recycle them. Canning lids are made from tin-plated steel covered with brass plating or a platinum finish. Call your local recycling company to see if tossing them in with cat food cans is safe or if they should be taken to a metal scrapyard.

BOILING WATER CANNER

Jars intended for boiling water bath canning can be processed in either a large enamel pot specifically designed for home canning or a large stockpot. Ideally, whatever vessel you choose should be deep enough to provide 1 to 3 inches (2.5 to 7.6 cm) of space above the jar lids, to accommodate both the boiling water itself and the attendant splashing. The enamel canning pots found in grocery and hardware stores often come with their own racks, which are metallic disks with handles. The purpose of a canning

An enamel stockpot

A pressure canner

rack is to keep the jars out of direct contact with the bottom of the pot, which would prevent water from circulating underneath the jars. The rack handles also allow you to raise and lower jars into the boiling cauldron with ease. If you are using a stockpot from your home collection and lack a rack, you can purchase one separately, or try fashioning one from either a round cake cooling rack or by attaching extra canning screw bands together with metal ties to form a circle. In lieu of handles to lift the entire rack out, use a jar lifter or tongs to individually remove jars from the canner.

PRESSURE CANNER

A pressure canner is a tall metal pot equipped with a locking lid containing a pressure-regulating gauge. This type of canner creates steam inside the pot, allowing temperatures of 240° to 250°F (115° to 121°C) to be reached. If you intend to can any low-acid foods, a pressure canner is absolutely essential. Don't even let yourself think that it might be possible to do otherwise. The risks posed by processing low-acid foods, unless pickled, in a boiling water bath are not worth it. Read more about low and high acid foods on page 24.

Pressure canners come in either weighted-gauge or dial-gauge models. Some models, like mine, actually have both dials and weighted gauges on their lids. Weighted-gauge pressure canners are fitted with a 5, 10, or 15-pound (2.25, 4.5, or 6.8 kg) pressure adjustment. These models allow small quantities of steam to escape from the lid every time the gauge whistles or rocks back and forth during processing. Altitude adjustments must be made on weighted-gauge pressure canners, as their accuracy is affected by changes in elevation. They are considered more durable, seldom requiring replacement or servicing. Dial-gauge pressure canners give exact numeric readings of the pressure inside the canner. If the pressure is too low or too high, raising or lowering the heat level of the burner adjusts it. Dial-gauge pressure canners must be checked annually for accuracy. This is often done at a local extension office, where you can check their instruments against your own. If a dial-gauge canner is giving incorrect pressure readings, it must be replaced.

LITTLE THINGS MEAN A LOT

While jars, lids, and canners are the most essential items needed to can food at home, a number of other kitchen items can speed up and simplify the process. Many of the items listed below can be found in most well-stocked kitchens. The first items on the list are the most specific to canning and, while not required, definitely help make the entire endeavor operate more smoothly.

KITCHEN SCALE Helpful for when recipes call for ingredients by the pound.

LID MAGNET Essentially a plastic stick with a round magnet attached to one end, lid magnets, or magnetic wands, as they are also known, make the task of fishing lids out of hot water considerably easier.

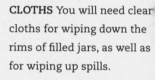

POTHOLDERS Be sure to have these nearby when lifting any heavy, hot, water-filled pots.

CLOTHS You will need clear cloths for wiping down the rims of filled jars, as well as for wiping up spills.

JAR LIFTER These resemble regular tongs, but the grabbing ends are covered in soft plastic. Not only do they make inserting and retrieving jars from boiling canners safer, but jar lifters also reduce the chance of scratching either the glass or the lid surface.

KITCHEN TIMER Setting a timer will take the guesswor out of how long your pot has been boiling.

CANNING FUNNEL Designed specifically to fit inside either narrow or wide-mouthed canning jars, these funnels help to keep messes and overfilling to a minimum.

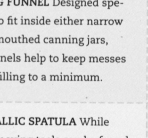

KNIVES A basic tool in any kitchen, knives in a variety of sizes are essential for processing foods for home canning.

NONMETALLIC SPATULA While bubble-removing tools can be found wherever canning supplies are sold, any long, thin, rubber spatula or wooden chopstick can be used for removing trapped air bubbles from filled jars.

MIXING BOWLS You'll need an assortment of bowls for holding prepared ingredients.

DRY AND LIQUID MEASURING CUPS A glass liquid measuring cup with a pouring spout can be an indispensable aid when transferring your cooked preserves from stovetop to jar.

MEASURING SPOONS For measuring out salt, spices, and so on.

CUTTING BOARD In addition to its more obvious role in chopping up fruits and vegetables, a cutting board is great for placing underneath jars while filling. It keeps the jars stationary and keeps spills off the counter.

FOOD MILL This less-common tool can be handy for puréeing apples for applesauce.

FOOD PROCESSOR This kitchen workhorse is truly wonderful when you have a good amount of slicing or chopping to do.

COLANDER For rinsing produce, draining off cooking liquid, and so on.

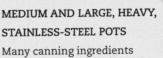

MEDIUM AND LARGE, HEAVY, STAINLESS-STEEL POTS Many canning ingredients are first cooked before being packed in jars, so having good-quality pots on hand is essential.

APPLE PEELER/CORER A countertop-mounted peeler saves vast amounts of time when you're peeling by the bushel.

LABELS You may think you have the memory of an elephant, but after canning all summer, remembering the contents of each jar can be daunting. Label and date what's what and when it was made.

MUSLIN TEA BAGS Used for creating herb bundles/sachets to prevent dried or loose herbs from direct contact with liquids. They're quite inexpensive and can often be found in stores where bulk herbs or teas are sold.

CHEESECLOTH A finely woven fabric used in home canning to either fashion into herb and spice sachets or separate solids from liquids in jelly-making.

JELLY BAG A cloth bag made of tightly woven cheesecloth, cotton flannel, or unbleached muslin used to strain solids from liquids. The bag is set into a 12-inch-high (30.5 cm) three-legged stainless-steel stand. The stand fits over the rim of a pot, thereby allowing juices to drip out and collect.

Chapter 3
Canning
Concepts

When it comes to starting out with home canning, it's really best to take things slowly. Aim for more of a water-creeping-up-your-swimsuit-slowly than a dive-right-in approach. While there are certainly amazing rewards to putting up foods yourself, those rewards can only be reaped when the correct steps and cautionary measures have been taken. So, brush up a bit on the fundamentals of canning before getting started. Once you know what to look for, you'll be that much more confident every time you break out the mason jars and fire up the stovetop!

CANNING CHEMISTRY 101

The world we humans inhabit keeps close quarters with a vast array of other living organisms. From the furry friends who share our homes to the microscopic life forms that live in our digestive tracts, many of these relationships and interactions are symbiotic. Microorganisms live in soil, in water, and in the air. While they are necessary and vital in their given functions, they do contribute to decay, especially when it comes to the deterioration of foods. Anyone who has had the immense displeasure of finding forgotten potatoes morphed into a gelatinous stew in the pantry has, regrettably, witnessed this natural deterioration firsthand.

Molds, yeast, and bacteria are, in most cases, the enemies of food preservation. Under controlled conditions, specific microorganisms can be welcome guests in the manufacture of wine, cheese, and pickles. Left to their own devices in canned goods, however, molds, yeast, and bacteria will render your food unsafe and inedible. Done properly, home canning stops these microorganisms in their tracks. By exposing them to heat and hermetically sealing glass jars, the little beasties are killed and the environment inside the jar becomes inhospitable to pathogen growth. Exposure to high temperatures also prevents naturally occurring enzymes present in food from speeding deterioration and decomposition. By killing off microorganisms and giving the kibosh to enzymes, home canning holds foods in a sort of suspended animation.

How does it work, exactly? Well, to begin, food is placed into a sterilized glass jar (more on sterilization ahead), capped with a 2-part flat lid and metal ring, and allowed to boil for a period of time, as directed by your recipe, in either a boiling water bath or a pressure canner. The heat makes the food and gases inside the jar expand, causing a buildup of internal pressure. Air begins to escape from the food and from the headspace, (see page 31) which is the area between the top of the food and the underside of the lid left unfilled, relieving this buildup of pressure. The buildup and release of gases recurs continually during the canning pro-

cedure, resulting in the formation of a vacuum inside the jar. As the jar cools, external pressure will be greater than the pressure inside the jar. The greater external pressure helps to keep the lid pushed down, while the compound surrounding the lid acts as glue, completely sealing in the contents of the jar and keeping hungry microorganisms out. Memorizing this process to expound upon at length at social gatherings is completely optional. What matters is that, if done properly, it keeps your lovingly preserved food from spoiling and keeps you from getting sick.

Fully processing foods according to directions is absolutely imperative. If any step is skipped, or done only partially, microorganisms may still be present inside the jar. Flavor can be compromised, your foods may spoil, and, of greatest concern, serious risks to health may be presented, including death! I say this not so that you bury your canning jars deep in the recesses of your basement in defeat, but instead to encourage you. Years of rigorous scientific research have resulted in tried-and-true, and inherently safe, home-canning methods, which you will learn about here. Done properly, you can feel confident that the fruits of your labor are safe for consumption.

A STERILE ENVIRONMENT

Perhaps you are a member of the club whose motto is "God made dirt and dirt don't hurt." Be that as it may, dirt, or more specifically, microorganisms in the environment, can be undesirable in home canning situations. If you are making any product that is to be processed in a boiling water bath for *less* than 10 minutes, you will need to sterilize your canning jars in addition to simply cleaning them.

To sterilize jars, place them upright on a canning rack inside a boiling water canner. Fill the canner with hot water, allowing water to flow into the empty jars, bring it to a boil, and process for 10 minutes. If you live at an elevation above 1000 feet (300 m), add 1 minute for each extra 1000 feet (300 m) above sea level (we'll discuss elevation in greater detail on page 27).

Once the required boiling time has been met, keep the jars in the canner with the lid on until you are just about ready to fill them. Using tongs, carefully remove the jars and drain the water back into the canner one at a time. This way the water in your canner will already be hot and ready to begin boiling again as soon as your jars are filled, fitted with lids, and returned to the canner for processing. Sterilization of canning jars is generally only required for items such as jams, jellies, and pickles. Any item requiring more than 10 minutes in a boiling water bath or that will be processed in a pressure canner does not need pre-sterilized jars.

ACID TEST

Knowing whether a food is low or high in acid is crucial to canning safety. This is because relative acidity determines the temperature at which microorganisms present on a food will be killed. The pH scale is used for measuring acidity. Those foods with a pH of 4.6 or lower are considered high acid, whereas those whose pH is above 4.6 are considered low acid. High-acid and low-acid foods will be processed differently.

Microorganisms on high-acid foods will be killed at 212°F (100°C), the temperature achieved by a boiling water bath. Microorganisms on lower-acid foods can survive at temperatures up to 240°F (116°C), so a boiling water bath cannot guarantee that pathogens on such foods will be destroyed. Pressure canning is an absolute must to ensure safety when canning low-acid foods.

Jams, jellies, chutneys, marmalades, butters, and most fruit spreads are generally higher in acid, and therefore may be processed in a boiling water bath. Some fruits, however, straddle the high/low acidity fence. For example, tomatoes can have variable acidity, and on occasion may have a pH higher than 4.6. Unless you plan on putting all your tomatoes to a litmus test, adding an acidifying agent like vinegar, lemon juice, or citric acid will provide enough acidity to allow tomatoes to be safely boiling water bath processed.

Otherwise, if you are intending to preserve any vegetable, meat, seafood, or poultry products through canning, they must be pressure canned. These foods are all low in acidity and therefore require a temperature of 240°F (116°C) in order to kill off spoilage-inducing microorganisms. The organism that poses the gravest concern to home canners is the bacterium *Clostridium botulinum*, also known as botulism toxin. This nasty beast, the cause of botulism food poisoning, can lurk in canned or bottled foods. Colorless, odorless, and tasteless, the spores of this microorganism are potentially lethal if consumed.

MIXING IT UP

So what if you want to make a product that combines both low and high-acid foods? Will you need to process through a boiling water bath or a pressure canner? The answer is pretty straightforward. If you are pickling or adding an acidifying agent to your recipe, then you're safe to use a boiling water bath. Otherwise, you'll need to fire up your pressure canner.

ACIDITY (PH) OF SELECT FRUITS AND VEGETABLES

Strong Acidity
0

2 — Plums (Damson and Blue)

3 — Apples, Apricots, Blackberries, Blueberries, Cherries, Gooseberries, Lemons, Peaches, Pears, Plums (Greengage, Red, and Yellow), Sauerkraut

4 — Tomatoes

4.6 — **Safety threshold**

5 — Asparagus, Beets, Cabbage, Carrots, Cauliflower, Celery, Eggplant, Green beans, Lima beans, Okra, Pumpkin, Spinach, Turnips

6 — Corn, Peas

14
Strong Alkalinity

(Data from the U.S. Food and Drug Administration, 2007)

Portrait of a Canner

Harriet

Expert in canning, quick pickling, fermenting, drying, freezing, and root cellaring, Harriet is a Jill-of-all-trades when it comes to food preservation. Along with her long-time friend Marge, she runs Preserve, a learning center in Portland, Oregon, dedicated to "teaching the art and science of food preservation." Originally from the Bronx, NY, Harriet ran a series of restaurants in Portland before partnering up with Marge to open Preserve.

Harriet cans extensively from her own garden, working diligently throughout the growing season to meet her family's food needs. In addition to preserving much of what she grows herself, she purchases from nearby farms. She's been at it for some time and advises those just getting into home canning to be realistic about the time and energy the technique necessitates: "Know why you are doing it, and be honest with the work it will require. This ain't no disco!" Clearly for Harriet, though, the extra work is well worth the yearlong payoff, made deliciously manifest in the form of homemade applesauce, relish, and canned tomatoes. 🥫

SIZING UP THE COMPETITION

I love to eat. You love to eat. Everything that lives loves to eat, including those organisms that want to eat whatever it is you're eating. Although you often can't see those other living entities (or, for our purposes, "beasts"), they are certainly there. From soil, air, water, and on every surface in between, microorganisms are moving along through their lives just as surely as you are through yours. Three classes of microorganisms pose health and quality concerns to canned foods: mold, yeast, and bacteria. Let us examine each and consider the ways in which they are affected by acidity and temperature.

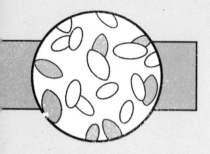

Mold

Mold is fairly easy to spot. No doubt you've found a patch greedily hugging the inside of a long-past-its-expiration-date container of cream cheese, or on a forgotten bit of zucchini buried in the bottom of the crisper drawer. Fuzzy and customarily green, gray, or white, mold is a type of fungus that grows in a multicellular filament. Molds prefer and thrive on high-acid foods such as fruits and pickles. Fortunately, they are destroyed at temperatures between 180 and 212°F (82 and 100°C), which is readily achieved in a boiling water bath.

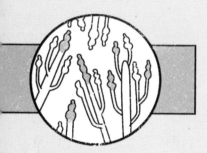

Yeast

Yeast is also a type of fungus. However, unlike molds that grow together in clusters, yeasts grow as single units. Many types of yeasts are highly valued in foods, as it is their presence that helps transform barley into a malty ale and grapes into a full-bodied Cabernet. This metamorphosis occurs as a result of yeast-induced fermentation. While fermentation is desirable in, say, converting cabbage into sauerkraut, it is not something you want occurring inside your canned goods. Yeasts are fond of high-acid foods, as well as those with ample sugar. Like molds, they will be destroyed in a boiling water bath.

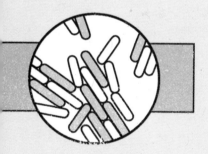

Bacteria

Bacteria are the most pernicious microorganisms of the lot. Temperatures that would easily cause molds and yeasts to bite the dust can actually be hospitable to bacteria. Some bacteria can even survive being boiled for a while in water. Worse yet, most bacteria are invisible to the naked eye. So while mold announces its presence as a fuzzy clump and yeast says "howdy do" with a pungent scent and tingly taste, bacteria can lurk, unnoticed, in your food. Salmonella and *Staphylococcus aureus* can cause food poisoning and general physical discomfort, but it's botulism that is the most menacing of bacterial threats to the home canner.

Clostridium botulinum doesn't particularly care for high-acid foods, and instead thrives in low-acid environments such as those found on vegetables, meats, seafood, and poultry. The one and only way to kill off *botulinum* spores naturally found on these low-acid foods is to process them in a pressure canner. This bears repeating, so I'll say it again. If you're canning any low-acid foods without pickling them, then you must use a pressure canner. I don't know about you, but when I go, I don't want it to be on account of a nasty critter lurking inside an unscrupulously packaged jar of green beans.

ALTITUDE ADJUSTMENT

As we move from sea level up to higher elevations, the temperature at which water boils changes. This occurs because of changes in surrounding atmospheric pressure. Essentially, the higher up you go, the less dense the air will be, and air with reduced density exerts less pressure. You know how your ears pop when flying in an airplane? That's because you have gone up in elevation and your body is recalibrating with the change in air pressure inside the cabin. So, at sea level, water will boil at 212°F (100°C), whereas on top of Mount Everest, it will boil at 156.2°F (69°C).

If you live at an elevation of over 1000 feet (300 m), you can't simply trust your eyes and assume that since the water is boiling, it must be above the temperature necessary to kill off molds and yeasts and to inactivate enzymes inside your jars. The truth is that it is boiling at a lower temperature, since it is responding to reduced air pressure. Whether you are using a boiling water bath or pressure canning, you will need to make adjustments if you live over 1000 feet (300 m) above sea level. Use the chart on page 126 to determine how much extra time you will need to tack on to the time suggested in the recipes in this book.

HOSTING A CANNING SWAP

Looking for a way to socialize and stock your pantry for winter? A canning swap is the way to go. You'll mix and mingle and savor your friends' and relatives' homemade wares, then part ways, each with a box of homemade delicacies. If hosted close to the holidays, the swap can double as a means of gathering items for gift giving.

Swap Planning Timeline

3 Months Ahead

Send out invitations, either by e-mail or snail mail. This may seem like an inordinately large amount of advance notice, but consider that most home canning occurs at the end of summer. If canners know they'll be making extra to share, they can plan their processing amounts accordingly. If you'd like to have a large turnout, consider asking your guests to invite friends of their own. Tell your invitees to plan on bringing at least as many jars of their item as there are people attending; that might be more than enough, but it sure beats having too few jars to go around. Encourage a variety of creative goods. Jams, jellies, relishes, and salsas made from exotic or unexpected ingredients are welcome, as are tried-and-true heirloom recipes.

3 Weeks Ahead

Send out a reminder, again, either via e-mail or regular mail. Ask guests to be sure to have all items labeled and dated. Everyone should bring a recipe card to place in front of their items so that guests can make selections according to dietary concerns or preferences.

1 Day Ahead

Make or purchase scones for sampling with the sweet spreads and tortilla chips and crackers for salsas and relishes. Be certain you have beverages on hand; coffee and tea are always welcome.

The Big Day

Dedicate a table for guests to display their wares. Consider separate tables for sweet and savory items if there are enough of each to merit doing so. Brew up some beverages, and get ready to gloat over your soon-to-be heavily laden pantry shelves!

The Methods

Now that you know the equipment you'll need to get started with home canning, we'll examine some of the methods used for getting the job done. The ingredients and end product will always dictate which technique is utilized. While many recipes will indicate what method is needed, it's good to be well acquainted with all the modes available for home processing. Make yourself something tasty to drink, find a quiet spot, and read over this chapter before you start mixing up a batch of marmalade or pickled okra. Here we'll explore boiled water bath and pressure canning.

 ## BOILING WATER BATH

The boiling water bath processing method is applied to high-acid foods including jams, jellies, marmalades, preserves, pickles, relishes, chutneys, salsas, ketchup, and some sauces. These items require a temperature of 212°F (100°C) in order to kill off harmful microorganisms, and the boiling water bath provides just such an environment. Follow these simple steps, and you'll be stocking your larder with delectable delights in no time!

1 Assemble all your equipment.

Gather up jars, lids and screw bands, canner and rack, jar lifter, funnel, spatula, recipe ingredients—everything you'll need to concoct your recipe, bottle it up, and process it. Doing so in advance saves you from last-minute scrambles. While you're at it, go ahead and read through your recipe. Know what you're getting into, how many jars it yields, and how much time you should be prepared to spend on the entire process.

2   Clean all jars, lids, and screw bands.

Give your gathered jars and their closures a good wash in hot, soapy water. Rinse them thoroughly, and set aside. Whether you are using brand-spanking-new jars or canning veterans, inspect the rims for cracks, nicks, or uneven edges. The easiest way to do this is by running your index finger around the circumference of the jar. Although it is unlikely that new jars will have faults, it is not entirely outside the realm of possibility. Weeding out the duds at this point will save you from leaks or jars that fail to seal properly. Check your screw bands, too. If you're reusing any, discard those that have rusted or show signs of wear such as scratches or scuff marks.

3   Heat the jars.

Fill your canner with enough water to cover the jars by 3 inches (7.6 cm). Depending on what sort of rack you are using, you can either put it into the canner at this point or fill it with jars and use the handles to lower it into the canner. Place your cleaned jars in the canner atop the rack, allowing the jars to become filled with water. It can be handy to have a teakettle with hot water ready in the event that you find yourself needing extra water to cover the jars once they have been submerged into the boiling water bath. Cover the pot and heat until almost boiling, around 180°F (82°C). Whatever you do, don't put cool jars into a boiling pot of water. By warming up the canning water and jars at the same time, you eliminate the risk of the jars cracking in response to a rapid change in temperature. Keep the jars hot and the canner covered until you are ready to begin filling. Alternatively, you can sterilize your jars in the dishwasher, but only if your model has a sterilization setting. **Note:** If you will be processing your jars for less than 10 minutes, then you will need to boil the jars for 10 minutes to sterilize them. Otherwise, just keep them warm, with the lid on.

TIP:

I can't tell you how many times I've been up to my elbows in jam and discovered I have fewer jars prepped than I have jam to fill them with. You really can't have enough "just in case" jars ready. If you end up not needing them after all, no harm done. Simply dry them off and store them back in your pantry. As far as extra lids go, though, I'd keep a "wait and see" approach. Once lids have been exposed to high heat, the sealing compound is activated and they shouldn't be used later. Monitor whether it looks like you might need an extra lid or two as you begin filling. If you do, simply submerge the new lids in the pot on the stove holding the other lids, and allow them to sit for several minutes before pulling them out and applying them to jars.

4   Prep the lids.

Fill a small pot with about 4 inches (10.2 cm) of water. Place the lids into the pot, cover, and heat until just simmering, around 180°F (82°C). Turn off the heat at this point and keep the pot containing the lids covered until you begin filling the jars. The screw bands don't need to be warmed up, just cleaned as described above and set aside until it's time to start filling the jars.

5   Prepare your recipe.

Work your magic on the stovetop, chopping, mixing, and cooking as your recipe indicates. If you're making a recipe with an especially lengthy cooking and preparation time, wait until you are finished, or at least on the home stretch, before you start warming up your jars and lids. Otherwise, you'll be using unnecessary energy keeping everything simmering the entire time.

6   Fill the jars.

Using a jar lifter or tongs, carefully remove one jar at a time from the canner, taking care to tip out the water away from you to avoid splashing.

Place the empty jar on a kitchen towel or wood cutting board on the counter. Any heat-protected surface will work. What you're looking to avoid is direct contact between a hot jar and a cold surface, such as a stone countertop, which could cause the jar to crack.

If your recipe has a pourable consistency, you may wish transfer the hot mixture into a pitcher or large glass meas ing cup with a pouring spout. This way, you can more easi and safely fill your jars with a minimum of mess.

Place a canning funnel over a jar, and fill the jar with you concoction until there is either ¼ inch (6 mm) or ½ inch (1. cm) of headspace, depending on what your recipe indicates Headspace is the space between the top of the food in the jar and underside of the lid. Generally, whole fruits and any pickled or acidified foods such as chutneys, relishes, pickles condiments, and tomatoes require ½-inch (1.3 cm) headspa while fruit spreads and juices need ¼-inch (6 mm) headspa Altitude has no effect on headspace requirements.

Using a nonmetallic spatula, a bubble releasing tool, or chopstick, release any trapped air bubbles inside the jar by running your tool of choice inside between the food and th jar. Trapped air bubbles can prevent proper sealing, creatin leaks and encouraging the growth of pathogens. After you have released any trapped air bubbles, check the headspac again and add or remove contents to adjust as needed.

TIP:

If you do end up scalding yourself, slather on some aloe ver pronto. It will help soothe the burn and expedite healing. O try this tip from my old days as a baker at a natural foods st and rub a few drops of lavender essential oil onto the burn.

Check Your Head(space)

Headspace accuracy is vital to creating a proper seal and for keeping your jar's contents inside where they belong. Too little room and the contents could spill out

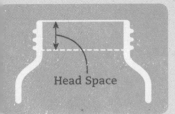

Head Space

when processing; too much air can prevent a complete seal from forming. Using a canning funnel definitely

helps, in my experience, as it serves as a visual gauge when the jar is getting full. If you are just getting started with home canning, know that the value of this simple step cannot be stressed enough.

Clean the jar rims.

Using a clean, dampened cloth or a paper towel, wipe the rim and threads of each jar, removing any food debris that may have dripped when filling. This step is very important, since food left on the jar rim can interfere with proper sealing.

8 Place the lids and screw bands on the jars.

Remove lids one at a time from their pot using either a magnetic jar lifter or tongs. Center a lid atop each jar, and secure with a screw band. Turn each screw band until you feel a little bit of resistance, and then continue twisting on until it is fingertip-tight. Don't overtighten the screw bands, since doing so can prevent the jars from venting properly during processing, which in turn can prevent a proper seal from forming.

10 Cool the jars.

After the processing time is complete, turn off the heat and take the lid off of the canner. Allow the jars to rest for 5 minutes, and then remove them one at a time using a jar lifter. Try to avoid tilting the jars as you remove them from the canner. Place the jars on a towel, and allow them to cool, untouched, for 24 hours. You might want to drape a kitchen cloth over your jars to keep them from catching drafts, which could cause the jars to cool too quickly, making them susceptible to cracking.

9 Process the jars.

Using a jar lifter, place your filled jars one at a time into the canner. Be certain they are sitting on top of the rack and aren't touching each other, since you want the boiling water to circulate underneath, over, and in between each jar. Once all of your jars are in, adjust the water level in the canner as needed to ensure that all jars are well covered. Place the lid on the pot, and bring the water to a rolling boil. Once a sustained boil is reached, you can begin timing. Processing times vary widely and are based on what type of food item you are preserving. Process for the amount of time specified in your recipe, adjusted for altitude if necessary (see Altitude Adjustment on page 126). The water must continue boiling rapidly for the entire duration of the processing. Check the water level periodically during processing, and add more boiling water as needed.

11 Check the seals.

Once your jars have had their cooling-off period, you'll want to ensure that they have sealed properly. If you heard lots of popping and pinging coming from your jars as they cooled, you're looking good, although you'll still need to determine whether each jar is sealed. Remove the screw bands from the jars, dry them thoroughly, and return them to the pantry. (Screw bands serve no immediate function after processing, and should be removed and stored to help prevent rusting caused by water drops between the screw band and the jar threads.) Dry off your jars completely, including the lid, threads, and body. Next, view your jars from the side, looking for a slight indention in the center of the lid. Press down on the lid with your fingertips and feel around for a downward curving dent. A properly sealed lid will remain

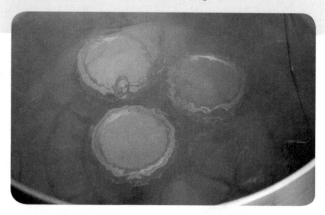

lace once you remove your finger, refusing to yield. Still
ot fully convinced? Grasp your jar by the lid only, checking
o see if it remains firmly attached. If your lid springs back
when pushed on, slips off either partially or completely,
hows no indentation, or displays a stream of tiny bubbles
nside (an indication that air is getting into the jar), you
ave a faulty seal.

2 Reprocess or refrigerate if needed.

hould one of your jars fail to seal properly, you can either
eprocess the jar and its contents, or set it aside for immedi-
te use. Reprocessing will compromise the quality of your
nished product, as the contents will have been subjected to
igh temperatures twice. Alternatively, you can simply put the
ar, unsealed contents and all, in the refrigerator and eat it up
vithin the week. If you opt to reprocess, you will need to begin
t the beginning, warming up the contents of your jar, cleaning
nd heating another jar, and using a new lid. Before you start,
hough, check the rim of the jar that failed to seal for nicks or
racks. If it's fine, go ahead and use the same jar again. Other-
vise, begin with a new jar. Next, fill the jar, check the head-
pace, remove air bubbles, and process again in the canner for
he amount of time specified in the recipe. If you have several
ad seals and don't have the time, energy, or temperament
o reprocess, simply empty the contents into freezer-proof
ontainers and freeze until needed. I wouldn't suggest freezing
ickles, though, as the amount of liquid they contain makes
hem less crunchy when returned to room temperature.

3 Label and store.

inally, label and date your jars while their contents are fresh
n your mind. Dating the jars is equally as important. When
you begin amassing an impressive arsenal of home-canned
goods, it will be necessary to know which need eating soon
and which can be left to stew in their own juices for a bit
onger. For the best flavor and texture, eat your wares within

one year. While those items older than one year might not have gone bad, their quality will begin to suffer. Many home canners use a permanent marker, writing directly on the lid for easy identification. You can also use labels and stickers if you'd like to adorn your goods for quick gift giving (see "Finishing Touches" page 37).

Store your jars in a cool, dry, dark location, such as a pantry or cabinet. If you're lucky enough to have a basement, you've hit the storage jackpot. Home-canned goods need to be kept between 40° and 70°F (4° and 21°C) in an area free from high humidity. If you are storing your jars in a garage and think the temperature out there might approach freezing, wrap the jars in newspaper or cloth, put them in a cardboard box, and cover the box with a blanket, providing an added layer of insulation against the cold. If your storage area reaches over 70°F (21°C) or is very humid, consider relocating your canned goods. Too much heat or humidity can cause seals to fail, resulting in spoilage.

Some items, such as tomato juice, might separate during storage. This is normal and no need for concern.

🍲 PRESSURE CANNER

All low-acid foods must be canned in a pressure canner, unless they have been acidified. The steps are similar to water bath canning but with a few unique twists. As discussed in Tools of the Trade, page 19, pressure canners come in either weighted- or dial-gauge versions. While the following directions apply to both models, always consult the manufacturer's directions provided with your model to ensure proper and safe use. If you picked up your pressure canner at a yard sale or via a no-longer-canning aunt, write or e-mail the manufacturer and request a manual, or simply check their website for an online version. Read it thoroughly before firing up your pressure canner for the first time.

2 Prep your pressure canner.

Put about 2 to 3 inches (5 to 7.6 cm) of water in the bottom of your pressure canner. Place the rack in the bottom of the canner. Begin warming the water over medium heat with the lid o

3 Clean and heat your jars and lids, prepare your recipe, fill the jars, clean the rims, and put on the lids and screw band

Refer to steps 2 through 8 of "Boiling Water Bath" for detaile instructions.

4 Exhaust the vent.

Take your filled jars and, using a jar lifter or tongs, place them one at a time into the pressure canner. Be certain they are sitting on top of the rack and aren't touching each other. Once all of your jars are in, place the lid on the canner and lock it into place according to the manufacturer's directions for your model. If using a dial-gauge canner, be sure

the petcock, the small tube sticking out of the lid, is open. I using a weighted-gauge canner, leave the weight off of the vent pipe. Bring water to a boil over medium-high heat. Onc you see steam coming out of the vent pipe, set a timer for 1 minutes. This process is known as *exhausting*. Its purpose is

1 Assemble all your equipment.

Gather up jars, lids and screw bands, canner and rack, jar lifter, funnel, spatula, recipe ingredients—everything you'll need to concoct your recipe, bottle it up, and process it. Read through your recipe. Know what you're getting into, how many jars it yields, and how much time you should be prepared to spend on the entire process.

force all the air inside of the canner out. You will want to ─ne this to be certain that you have allotted 10 minutes and ─ less, as failure to do so could alter temperatures inside ─e canner and result in improperly sealed jars. Exhausting ─necessary every time you use a pressure canner.

Process the jars.

─ter you have exhausted the vent ─ 10 minutes, close the petcock on ─al-gauge canners by putting the ─unterweight on it. For weighted- ─uge canners, close the vent by ─acing the weight over the vent ─pe. If you are at sea level up ─ 1000 feet (300 m) elevation, position the weight at the ─mber (5, 10, or 15) indicated by your recipe. If you are more ─an 1000 feet (300 m) above sea level, refer to "Altitude Ad- ─stment" (page 126) and amend canner settings accordingly. ─epending on the model you are using, you will either watch ─e dial until it reaches the desired pressure (dial-gauge) or ─ten and watch for the weight to begin to jiggle and sputter ─d rock (weighted-gauge), indicating pressure has been ─ached. Once that level is achieved, set a timer for the num- ─r of minutes listed in your recipe.

It is essential that the pressure in your canner remain ─nstant during processing. Significant fluctuations can ─use food inside the jars to leak out, ruining the seals in ─e process. You will therefore need to keep an eye on your ─nner for the entire duration of the processing time. Dial- ─uge models should read at the same number the entire ─me, and weighted-gauge models should continue to emit ─ hissing sound and jiggle one to four times per minute. If ─mething takes you away from the stovetop and you return ─ find a reduction in pressure, you will have to start timing ─om the beginning. The only way to ensure food safety, and ─event the dreaded botulism, is to guarantee that you have ─ocessed your items at the correct pressure for the full ─uration of the suggested time.

6 Cool down the canner.

Once you are absolutely certain that your canner has con-tinually remained at the correct pressure and your process-ing time is complete, turn off the heat and allow the canner to cool. When the pressure gauge returns to zero (consult the instructions included with your model to deter-mine when this occurs), it is then safe to remove the weight from the vent. Do not remove the weight, however, before the pres-sure returns to zero. De-pending on your model, it could take between 15 minutes and one hour for the canner to cool completely and pressure

to reach zero. After you take off the vent, wait another few minutes (again, refer to your model's instructions) before removing the lid. As you take the lid off, be certain to tip the steamy side up away from you, as the steam that will rise out of the canner, along with any water droplets accumulated on the underside of the lid, will be very hot.

7 Remove the jars.

Using a jar lifter or tongs, remove the jars one at a time. Try to avoid tilting the jars as you remove them from the canner. Place the jars on a towel, and allow them to cool, untouched, for 24 hours. You might want to drape a cloth over your jars to keep them from catching drafts.

8 Check the seals, reprocess if necessary, label, and store.

Refer to steps 11 to 13 of "Boiling Water Bath" for detailed instructions.

THE HOME CANNING CANON

- Use the boiling water bath processing method for high-acid foods only.

- Process low-acid foods in a pressure canner, unless you acidify them.

- Always check jars for nicks or scratches before use.

- Be certain your equipment and preparation areas are thoroughly cleaned between each use.

- Leave the amount of headspace per jar as indicated in the recipe.

- Use new lids each time. A used lid cannot be trusted to seal properly.

- Only begin timing processing once the water surrounding your submerged, filled jars is at a rapid boil or your pressure canner has emitted steam for 10 minutes.

- Don't use jars larger than 1 quart (.95 L). It is more difficult to guarantee the contents of larger jars have been uniformly heated during processing.

- Adjust for altitude when necessary.

- Always follow recipes to the letter. Adding even just one ingredient can alter the pH.

- Examine used screw bands for signs of wear before use.

- If a lid fails to seal, remember the two Rs: Reprocess or Refrigerate. Freezing is another option if your entire batch failed to seal and you're not quite feeling up to the task of processing the whole thing over again.

- Never use a dishwasher to sterilize jars unless your model has a sterilization setting.

- Avoid temperature fluctuations between your jars, their contents, and hard surfaces, as this may cause the jars to crack.

Portrait of a Canner

Jenny

Juggling caring for a young toddler with a career in nonprofit work and documentary filmmaking, Jenny is no stranger to the hectic demands of modern living. Even still, she's decided to include home canning in her culinary practices, firing up the canner up to 8 times during the summer. Although she grew up with a jam-making grandmother and great-aunt, it was her desire to support local foods that really got her canning seriously. "My husband and I planted and grew enough tomatoes last summer so that we could can a large enough quantity to take us through the winter and spring. The alternative would have been to purchase tomatoes flown in from Italy or California. We prefer to know where and how our food is grown and, by the same token, reduce the carbon footprint wherever we can."

Jenny sources the majority of what she preserves from her home garden. A bumper crop of cucumbers and radishes have led to some inspired pickles, while the tomato harvest provided her family with enough to enjoy fresh over the summer and plenty extra to put up several dozen quarts for use later. She encourages those who have never canned before to try their hand at the technique. "It's much easier than you think it is! It is also much safer than common wisdom would have it. All kinds of people have been canning for 200 years without any major issues."

FINISHING TOUCHES

If you intend to give away any of your canned goods, there are numerous options for dressing up the jars in gift-worthy garb. Wax seals, labels, ribbon, raffia, and decorative cloth are but a few of the ways in which your jars can go from functional to fabulous.

Cloth, Paper, and Scissors

Quickly transform your jars with handmade paper, printed paper, or fabric. Using straight-edged craft scissors or decorative-edged scissors, cut a circle of paper or cloth 1/2 to 1 inch (1.3 to 2.5 cm) larger than the circumference of the jar you wish to decorate. Secure the cloth or paper to the lid with ribbon, raffia, twine, or whatever your imagination suggests. You can also use inexpensive wax or parchment paper for jar toppers with great results.

A Fashionable Label

Labels (page 21) are another way to gussy up your jars in minutes. You can pick up blank labels at an office supply store, and design labels to your liking on your home computer. Alternatively, you could search for preprinted labels with space to handwrite information about the jar's contents. Canning-appropriate labels can be found online on sites such as Etsy.com or MyOwnLabels.com, where you can custom-design labels. Round, metal-rimmed tags are a simple yet unexpected way to festoon your wares. There are no limitations when it comes to labeling your jars. Just remember to include the date in addition to a description of the contents.

Slow Food

Founded in Rome in 1986 by Carlo Petrini, Slow Food is an international movement seeking to preserve global food cultures and food diversity. The movement developed as a response to the rapidly growing international presence of fast food chains. Championing the position that food must be good (in terms of flavor), clean (produced in an ecologically responsible manner), and fair (each person involved in its production must be treated ethically and humanely), Petrini's fledgling movement has quickly grown to include members in 122 countries. Slow Food proponents include chef Alice Waters, author and journalist Michael Pollan, and author Eric Schlosser.

Home canning undoubtedly meets the criteria for a "slow" food. Sure, canning fruits and vegetables yourself takes longer than picking up provisions at the grocery store, thereby making it slow in a temporal sense, but it's also slow in that by preserving the bounty of a harvest at the end of the growing season, resources are conserved. Instead of buying applesauce or blackberry jam made from fruit that may have been grown thousands of miles away, home canning allows you to both eat locally and cheat the seasons by devouring that blackberry jam while a heavy snow blankets the ground. So you can see how home canning upholds the "clean" aspect of Slow Food principles. Home canning also possesses the capacity to be fair, especially if the ingredients selected are grown organically, purchased through a local farmers' market, or are sourced from businesses promoting fair-trade practices. Lastly, items canned at home taste good, the final component of the Slow Food mission. When you're able to control the flavorings and use the freshest produce available, the texture, aroma, and flavor of your final product is unmatched.

YOU, TOO, CAN CAN:
Hosting an At-home Canning Party

Come summertime, when the bounty of the season threatens to overwhelm your garden, and the tables at the farmers' market creak and groan under the weight of their offerings, consider hosting a canning get-together. Those already schooled in the trade can share tips and advice, while newbies will gain invaluable hands-on experience. Limit the number of guests so that everyone's wares can get cooked on the stovetop space available. Or, you could invite loads of friends and turn the gathering into a sleepover, burning the midnight oil as you toil over simmering pots and sizzling pressure canners. Depending on what you're making, you could even sample some of your creations for breakfast the next morning.

Party Planning Timeline

Three Weeks Ahead

Send invitations via e-mail or regular mail. For the sake of time, you will want to limit the number of guests to no more than six; alternatively, you could simply have all guests make the same recipe, with each person performing a different task in the kitchen. Decide if you'd like guests to arrive with their ingredients, or if you'd like to include a trip to a nearby farmers' market or U-pick farm as part of the day's activities. Ask guests to come with a recipe and jars for making their items. Ask guests to share in advance what recipe they will be preparing, to avoid duplications.

One Day Ahead

Prepare appetizers or a small meal for your guests to nosh on. Have your kitchen clean and ready for cooking up a storm!

The Big Day

Assemble all your equipment, and be sure it is completely clean. Share in the work as you chop, cook, and can, sending each guest home with several jars worth of whatever is put up during the event.

The Science of Sugar

More than simply making your preserves taste sweet, sugar plays a critical role in making your jam, well, jam. That is to say, without the right amount of sugar in a recipe, you'll have a runny goo on your hands, not a firm, stable spread. This is because of the chemical interaction that occurs when sugar and fruit pectin get together. Pectin is a type of polysaccharide, which is a complex carbohydrate. When the pectins in whatever fruit you are using interact with sugar, chemical bonds are formed that bolster the stability and smoothness of the mixture.

Sugar also serves as a natural preservative. This happens because sugar is hygroscopic, meaning it pulls moisture out of the air. In home canning, this is desirable, since any moisture that is drawn into the sugar molecules means less moisture available in the jar for microorganisms to invade and contaminate. Whether you are using granulated sugar or sugar syrup made from fruit juice, be sure to use the proper amount indicated in a recipe to prevent the mold brigade from feasting on your carefully crafted preserves before you do!

The Science of Salt

While salt is used primarily for flavor when canning vegetables, it is essential to quality, texture, and safety when home-canning seafood, quick pickles, and fermented foods.

Salt is made up of the chemicals chloride and sodium. Like sugar, salt is hygroscopic, pulling water out of the air and into itself. This happens through the process of osmosis, a type of diffusion causing solutes to move from an area of high water concentration (such as a diluted solution) to one of low water concentration (such as a concentrated solution). A salty brine has a lower concentration of water than the water present inside the cells of a vegetable such as a cucumber, causing the water inside the cuke to flow out. When this principle is applied to pickling, salt helps pickles be crunchier, as the water and moisture that would otherwise flow into them is being drawn instead into the salt molecules.

Salt also acts as a preservative. In addition to pulling moisture out of foods, salt pulls moisture away from bacteria, making it difficult for them to survive. Undesir-

able beasties are killed off, keeping your pickles safe until you're ready to eat them. When making fermented foods, salt is absolutely vital. While salt discourages some bacteria, it encourages the growth of others that are desirable, such as lactic acid bacteria. This type of bacteria is a group of related bacteria that produce lactic acid as the result of carbohydrate fermentation. It is lactic acid that gives pickles their characteristic puckery twang. When salt is at a certain concentration in a solution, lactic acid grows more abundantly and more quickly than any other bacteria present. If there is too little salt in a solution, other bacteria may thrive and outcompete lactic acid for survival, spoiling your pickles in the process. Too much salt and the lactic acid isn't able to really do its thing, leaving your vegetables unpickled.

Portrait of a Canner

Rachel

A profound love of fruit, most notably when it is incorporated into dessert, is what brought Rachel to jam making. An avid baker of desserts for as long as she can remember, she found herself "fascinated with the plethora of fruits available" in California's Bay Area farmers' markets after moving there in the late 1990s. It was during one of her market excursions that Rachel decided to experiment with making jam, having grown up with her mother's rhapsodic raspberry jam, made with berries from their backyard. Although her jam trials didn't immediately produce the results she'd hoped for, it sparked in her a desire to perfect the process of jam and marmalade making until it matched her "aesthetic vision of what jam should be."

This simple yearning to create jam the way she thought it should be made, as well as the jam she wanted but couldn't find in stores, would soon blossom into a business, Blue Chair Fruit Company. Each batch of jam at Blue Chair is handmade in small batches using French copper jam kettles. This method employs an age-old tradition of artisanal fruit preserving. Rachel's company uses seasonal fruits, flowers, and flavorings, locally grown and sustainably produced. Offerings can change from year to year, depending on what is available.

Now adept at producing her own enticingly creative jams, such as strawberry marsala with rosemary or bourbon-laced Seville orange marmalade with star anise, Rachel has advice to dispense for those interested in getting on board the jam wagon. "The number one thing I would tell people is: always cook small batches, and always use a wide pan. Also, only use the best fruit for preserves." Coming from someone who's been hovering over a copper kettle four to six days a week for going on 10 years, we'd all do well to listen up.

Chapter 4
Ingredients

Experienced cooks know that a dish is really only as good as its ingredients. You can't expect stellar results from subpar supplies. For a recipe to end up spectacular, it must begin with the best quality ingredients you can find. It might take a little more time, as you learn to carefully select the most ideal specimens, but I'd argue that the extra five minutes required to find the ripest, smoothest peaches for a batch of buttery, fragrant jam is well worth it.

NATURAL SELECTION

In an ideal world, every fruit, vegetable, herb, and spice would be available only in its purest, cleanest, most natural form. The world in which we live, however, is far from ideal. Unless you grow your food yourself and are aware of its treatment during its entire life cycle—from seed, to germination, growth, and harvest—you will have to rely on labeling to make informed food purchases.

Organic foods are grown without the use of toxic pesticides and fertilizers. Such foods must be free of antibiotics, artificial growth hormones, genetically modified organisms (GMOs), irradiation, and sewage waste. Furthermore, the production of organic foods cannot involve the use of cloned animals, artificial ingredients, or synthetic preservatives.

In the United States, federally mandated standards require that third-party state or private agencies oversee organic certification for producers. The U.S. Department of Agriculture (USDA) in turn accredits these agencies. In order for a farm to become certified organic, the land must not have had any prohibited materials applied to it for three years. Scrupulous records must be on hand to prove this, in addition to a detailed plan for preventing contamination by prohibited substances. Outside the U.S., a number of agencies perform similar organic certification testing around the world. Requirements, regulations, and oversight vary from country to country but are, for the most part, quite similar.

Why search out organic ingredients for home-canned goods? Put simply, they're healthier—for you, your family, and your planet. Research indicates organically grown foods are higher in a number of nutrients, containing more vitamin C, iron, magnesium, phosphorus, and antioxidants than their conventionally grown counterparts. Furthermore, foods grown organically yield greater amounts of omega-3 fatty acids and conjugated linoleic acid (CLA). These essential fatty acids are necessary in order for the immune, cardiovascular, reproductive, and nervous systems to function optimally. Since your body can't manufacture essential fatty acids on its own, they must be obtained through the diet.

Finally, organically grown foods simply taste better. Take celery, for example. The conventionally grown version most people are familiar with has an acrid and somewhat bitter aftertaste. Organic celery is sweet, crunchy, and delicious. It's just one example of how the absence of artificial pesticides and fertilizers is truly manifest in the flavor of many organically grown foods.

Not too long ago, organic foods weren't terribly easy to come by. Today, however, as consumers gain more information about the detrimental effects of toxic agents on their health, the demand for organics has increased. From local grocery stores, food co-ops, farmers' markets, and even big-box retailers, organic foods are not hard to find. For many, though, the cost of organic foods may be out of reach. While organic foods do not have to be more costly than those that are conventionally produced, many organic options currently are. As demand continues to grow, the price will fall. In the meantime, acquaint yourself with those foods whose conventionally grown versions tend to contain the highest levels of pesticide residue and should always be purchased organic. Other foods tend to be generally low in pesticide application even when conventionally grown, and these may be a lower priority to buy organic.

According to the Environmental Working Group (EWG), a nonprofit organization dedicated to using public information to promote public health and environmental protection, the following items, dubbed the "Dirty Dozen," show the greatest traces of pesticides:

"Dirty Dozen"		
	apples	peaches
	celery	pears
	cherries	potatoes
	grapes	spinach
	lettuce	strawberries
	nectarines	sweet bell peppers

The following produce items were shown to contain the smallest amounts of pesticides, designated by the EWG as the "Cleanest 12":

"Cleanest 12"		
	asparagus	kiwifruit
	avocados	mango
	bananas	onions
	broccoli	pineapple
	cabbage	sweet corn (frozen)
	eggplant	sweet peas (frozen)

These results were based on 43,000 tests for pesticide levels conducted by the U.S. Department of Agriculture (USDA) and the U.S. Food and Drug Administration (FDA). You can download a wallet-sized version of this list from EWG's website, www.ewg.org. As a nutrition consultant, I like to keep copies of this list available for clients who want to go organic but just can't afford to make the switch completely. I find myself returning to my own copy, safely tucked into my wallet, again and again.

PROPERLY SEASONED

I was at my local grocer the other day and found fresh strawberries and blueberries, carefully cradled in plastic clamshells, in the produce department. While that discovery seems rather innocuous, what makes it noteworthy is that it was January.

January! While the first month of the year is associated with many things, among them winter squash, iced-over windshields, resolutions, and hot chocolate, it is generally not associated with fresh berries—at least not in the northern hemisphere. Innovations in transportation and refrigeration technologies have made some foods available without regard to their traditional growing seasons. While that might be an ideal advancement for things like Earl Grey tea, dark chocolate, and vanilla beans, for others, especially perishable items, it can mean compromised flavor, as well as a reduction in nutrients.

Foods grown in far-flung locales must be picked before they are fully ripe in order to allow for transit time. As soon as any produce item is harvested, it begins to lose nutrients. Pick any fruit or vegetable and consider the days that have elapsed from harvest, to packaging, transit, and finally shelf time once it reaches the grocery store. When those New Zealand apples reach Iowa in March or a cluster of Chilean grapes shows up at your market in Maine during a New England nor'easter, many of the nutrients originally present are either greatly reduced or nearly gone. Why spend your hard-earned money on foods that in theory seem nutritious, only to have them depleted of so many of the health benefits you're eating them for?

Every season naturally offers a bounty of delicious foods. Nothing compares to cooling strawberries, freshly picked, in the heat of summer, or a hearty bowl of root vegetable soup bringing comfort on a cold winter night. Eating in season offers unrivaled flavor in addition to complete nutrients. Don't think of it as depriving yourself. Instead, consider eating seasonally to be the most culinarily rewarding act possible. When you eat seasonally, you eat the best available. In my book, that trumps lackluster midwinter strawberries every time!

CLOSE TO HOME

Inextricably linked with eating seasonally is eating locally. Yes, it is possible to find apples at your local grocer that were grown 3000 miles (4800 km) away even when they are in season in your area. You can also find corn shipped in from several states over at the same time you see it crowding the fields of nearby farms. Trucked-in produce is lacking more than just flavor. Those foods, while technically in season where they originated, were harvested before peak ripeness in order to be shipped. Precious nonrenewable resources were used to transport produce that could be easily found at your local farmers' market, U-pick farm, or, even better, in your own backyard. (Talk about local!) What's more, eating locally allows you to meet the people who grow your food. You can ask them direct questions about how they grew the goods they're offering. Carrots in a plastic sack at the store don't answer back.

Eating locally also creates a viable market for small farmers, who, tragically, are a dying breed. In fact, the number of individuals currently employed in farming in the U.S. is so low that it is no longer listed as a vocation with the Census Bureau. That's set to change, though, as increasing numbers of young people, concerned about environmental stewardship and healthy foods, are literally entering the field. When you purchase your foods from a local supplier, you provide a reliable customer base for them while ensuring nutritious, delicious foods for yourself and your family.

Eating and buying locally produced foods is an amazing way to meet and connect with your wider community. Some farmers put aside items they know particular customers would appreciate, while others even keep treats on hand for canine companions. I can't think of a more ideal means of obtaining the best possible ingredients for home canning use and making some new friends in the process.

INCREDIBLE EDIBLES

If you want your home-canned goods to be sublime, you truly must begin with the best available ingredients. When searching for ideal produce, be on the lookout for items that are ripe and free from blemishes and bruises. Bear those criteria in mind at all times. You want your fruits and vegetables to be at their peak of ripeness and in the best condition possible. If you find that the ingredients you were hoping to use are past their prime or show signs of wear, it's best to simply count your losses and either eat them fresh or cook and eat them straightaway. Many organically grown fruits and vegetables can be less "perfectly" shaped than their conventionally grown counterparts, which is fine. What you want to avoid, though, is signs of wear or aging. For example, when purchasing some locally grown apples intended for apple butter, I left behind those with visible bruises, worm holes, and cuts. Those apples would be fine for an apple crisp or slathered with peanut butter; they're just not the right choice for home canning.

Take care that your fruit isn't overripe, either, as that can affect pectin levels. Overripe fruit can also make a mushy mess, especially if you're attempting to can fruits in whole form. If you are harvesting the produce yourself, try not to stack the fruits on top of each other, as this can cause bruising. Instead, lay them out flat in a basket or even a cardboard lid. Be especially careful if you are harvesting soft fruit such as berries, cherries, and stone fruits such as peaches. If they are at peak ripeness they can crush quite easily. If you're going to go to all the trouble of getting tangled up with thorns (berries) and ladders (cherries and stone fruits), you really don't want to be crushing the goods on their way back to your kitchen. You'll also want to give your produce a gentle scrub

and washing before use. Wait until you're ready to begin your recipe before you do this, though, to ensure no lasting damage results should you have a less than gentle hand.

Never use waxed produce items such as shiny, glossy apples or cucumbers for home canning. The wax affects flavor and is hard to remove, which makes it difficult for liquid to penetrate while pickling. If an acid, such as lemon juice or vinegar, is not able to fully penetrate a low-acid item, dangerous bacteria can develop if processed only in a boiling water bath.

Not every produce variety is optimally suited for home canning. Some varieties simply hold up to the rigors of processing better than others. At the grocery store, rarely will varietal names be listed except for sturdy fruits like apples and pears. Some farmers' market sellers do list the specific names of what they've grown. If you don't see what you're looking for, don't be afraid to ask. Many farmers can easily tell you the name of the cucumbers or peppers they are selling.

If you plan to grow your own produce, seek out canning-worthy varieties. Ask your local County Extension agent for recommendations on good varieties of produce to can. In the United States, all counties have agents available for answering a wide range of agricultural questions. You can find yours online or in the phone book under state listings. Abroad, local farmers, universities, and agricultural organizations would be good resources for produce-related questions.

Use the following list as a guide for selecting produce variet[ies] known to hold up well when canned. These varieties work equ[ally] well whether you are putting up fruits and vegetables whole o[r] incorporating them into condiments. Consider this guide as su[g]gestive, not definitive or comprehensive. The varieties of produ[ce] available to the home gardener are truly endless. Consult your seed catalog and feel free to experiment.

Fruit

Apples: Golden Delicious, Granny Smith, Gravenstein, McIntosh, Newton, Pippin, Winesap

Apricots: Blenheim, Early Gold, Moongold, Royal

Cherries: Bing, English Morello, Golden Sweet, Meteor, Montmorency, Royal Ann, Windsor

Citrus: Most citrus withstands canning without problem[s]

Figs: Black Mission, Brown Turkey, Celeste, Everbearing, Kadota, King, Magnolia

Grapes: Concord (seedless), Flame, Reliance, Thompson

Peaches: Belle of Georgia, Champion, Elberta, Golden Jubil[ee], Madison, Red Haven, White Heath

Pears: Bartlett, Duchess, Kieffer, Moonglow

Plums: Burbank, Greengage, Laroda, Mariposa, Mount Roy[al], Santa Rosa, Satsuma, Seneca, Stanley

Vegetables

Beets: Big Red, Detroit Supreme, Little Ball, Red Ace, Ruby [Queen]

Black-eyed Peas: Queen Anne

Butter Beans: Dixie

Carrots: Falcon II, Minicor, Little Finger

Corn: Flavor Queen, Golden Jubilee, Merlin

Cucumbers: Amour, Diamant, Northern Pickling

Lima Beans: Fordhook 242

Okra: Annie Oakley II, Cajun Delight, Red Velvet

Peas: Alaska Early, Alderman

Peppers: Anaheim, Cherry Sweet, Jalapeno M, Super Red Pi[mento]

Tomatoes

Crushed: Amish Paste, Bellstar

Soup: Bellstar, Roma, Ropreco, San Marzano, Super Fantas[tic]

Whole: Glamour, Halley, Heinz 1350 VF, Marglobe, Ole, Red [...]

OU SAY TOMAYTO, I SAY TOMAHTO

matoes hold a special place in the world of home canning. ot only are they canned more than any other item, they are cceptionally versatile and take well to processing. In fact, the ily tomato varieties that aren't so keen on being canned are ape and cherry tomatoes. When you consider there are over 500 members of the *Solanum lycopersicum* species out there, at restriction shouldn't crimp your style.

Tomatoes were once considered a reliably high-acid food, id processing in a boiling water bath was the preferred route putting them up. That's no longer the case. The growing en- ronment of tomatoes, influenced by fluctuations in weather id soil composition, their maturity level at time of sale, and ormal differences between tomato varieties is so variable that any end up straddling the low/high-acid fence. As a result, is suggested that an acidifying agent be added to tomatoes alter their pH. Lemon juice or citric acid are the customary iditives, as vinegar can alter the flavor. If you want to put up batch of balsamic-infused tomatoes, however, then vinegar ill certainly do the job. No additional acid is needed when nning tomatillos and green tomatoes, as they are naturally gh-acid.

The USDA notes that use of a pressure canner will result in gher quality and more nutritious canned tomato products.

When deciding which type of tomatoes to use, consider your cipe. Are you canning tomatoes that will eventually be made to sauce? If so, go for plum tomatoes, as they're generally ss juicy, making them ideal for thick, hearty marinaras. If u'll be using your canned tomatoes in salsa, round fruit will ork just as well as plum.

Acidifying Tomatoes

Lemon juice: 1 tablespoon per pint

Citric acid: 1/4 teaspoon per pint

For quarts, simply double the amount of acidifying agent.

Bottled lemon juice is preferable as it has a more consistent pH than fresh-squeezed, which can vary from one fruit to the next.

SUGAR AND SPICE AND EVERYTHING NICE

While it is possible to put up fruit and vegetables with nothing more than added liquid, many home canners elect to jazz up their provisions, creating culinary concoctions rivaling the finest store-bought goods. Below we'll explore some of the common, and not so common, additives every home canner should know about.

Sweeteners

Sugar

Sugar is essential for jelling jams, jellies, marmalades, and chutneys. It interacts with pectin and acid to give preserves body and prevent runniness. Additionally, sugar acts as a preservative, preventing spoilage. Without adequate sugar in a recipe, the shelf life of a home-canned item is seriously compromised.

Most recipes calling for sugar require regular granulated white sugar, as it is neutral in both taste and color. In my

home canning, I use organic cane sugar. The texture is the same as granulated white sugar, but organic cane sugar is less refined, retaining more vitamins and minerals. Brown or muscovado sugars are best for use in chutneys and darker marmalades, as their brown hue and molasses flavor can mask colors and flavors in more subtle recipes. Superfine sugar, also known as caster sugar, is sometimes called for in curd recipes. Curds require low heat, and superfine sugar is perfect for dissolving quickly at low temperatures, due to the small size of the sugar granules. If you cannot locate superfine sugar, whip up some of your own by pulsing granulated sugar in a food processor or blender for several seconds.

Honey

Honey can be used as a sweetener in homemade preserves where its distinct flavor is welcome. Honey contains moisture not found in granulated sugar, and for this reason preserves made with honey will generally have a softer texture, not firming up quite as well as those made with granulated sugar. That said, if honey is your favorite sweetener and you don't care if it masks the gentle flavors of the fruit it is mixed with, then by all means use it. Honey is more dense than granulated sugars, so it cannot be substituted cup-for cup. Instead, replace every 1 cup of sugar with ⅞ cup of honey, a don't alter any other liquid amounts in the recipe.

Fruit Juice

It's possible to reduce the amount of granulated sugar in recipes considerably by using fruit juice concentrates. Most often, 100 percent apple, pineapple, or white grape juice is used to replace most or all of the sugar called for in traditional sugar-based recipes. However, as sugar acts as a thickening agent, re pes made exclusively with fruit juice as a sweetener will need added pectin. The one exception is when the recipe is compos almost entirely of high-pectin fruits; for example, an all-fruit recipe for apple butter. Do not attempt to alter existing recipes calling for granulated sugar. Instead, seek out those written expressly for fruit juice-based sweetening. Several companies now offer a "no-added-sugar pectin," allowing low-sugar recip to successfully gel. Many include recipes on the box itself.

If you wish to can whole fruit, fruit juice is a wonderf natural sweetener that can used in place of a sugar syru Be sure to pick mild-flavored juices for this purpose, as anything with too pronounc a taste might end up maskin the fruit itself. White grape juice or apple juice work we

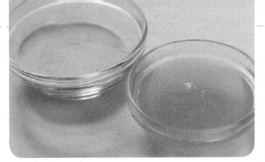

Pectin

Pectin is a naturally occurring, water-soluble type of carbohydrate that is found in the tissue, skin, and seeds of fruit. It reacts with sugar and acid to create a gel, or bond. Without it, your exquisite strawberry jam would be little more than a runny red puddle. Fruits contain varying degrees of inherent pectin, ranging from low to high (see "Pectin Portion"). While under-ripe fruits contain more pectin, they are inferior in flavor and are not recommended.

If you are cooking with a high-pectin fruit, such as apples, adding additional pectin might be unnecessary. When cooking a low-pectin fruit, it is normally possible to achieve a gel without added pectin, simply by cooking for a longer duration. This doesn't always work, however, and extra pectin may be required, either by the addition of a high-pectin fruit or incorporating commercial pectin. Care must be taken, however, as pectin is a fickle muse, deteriorating quickly if a fruit is too ripe or if it is allowed to cook for too long. In addition to breaking down pectin content, prolonged cooking can result in a darkened color and diminished flavor.

Commercial Pectin

Made from tart apples or the pith found under the peel of citrus fruit, commercial pectin is 100 percent natural. It is available in both powdered and liquid forms. Powdered pectin is incorporated into a recipe before cooking, whereas liquid pectin is generally incorporated into the fruit and sugar mixture after it has been heated. Prepared pectin is also available in low and no-sugar forms, enabling you to control the amount of sugar added to a recipe and still achieve a firm gel. Commercial pectin supplies will need to be replenished annually, as they don't hold up well over time.

Homemade Pectin

Making your own pectin from fruit is a great step toward food self-sufficiency. That said, it is also a time-consuming process producing a perishable item. Sour apples are the source of choice for making homemade pectin. You will need to verify that the apples used in your recipe are fresh, as pectin content decreases with age. Don't just assume apples in the produce section of your local market were recently harvested, especially if they aren't from a local source. Ask the produce manager, or only make homemade pectin in autumn, when apples are in season. If you have your own apple trees or a nearby U-pick farm, pectin production might be an ideal way to make use of a bushel or a peck.

Making Your Own Pectin

You can make as much or as little pectin as you would like. One pound of apples will yield around 1 pint of pectin. When choosing apples, the more tart varieties are preferable.

Wash the apples and then cut them into quarters. Be sure to hang onto the core and peel, as these parts contain high amounts of pectin. Place the apples into a stainless-steel pot. Add 2 cups of water and 1 tablespoon bottled lemon juice for each pound of apples.

Bring to a boil, then reduce the heat, cover, and simmer for 35 to 40 minutes, stirring occasionally to prevent the apples from sticking to the bottom of the pan.

Remove from heat. Drain the mixture through a large sieve, removing solid pieces; discard the solids. Next, strain the apple liquid through either a jelly bag or several damp layers of cheesecloth. Return the strained liquid to a stainless-steel pot, heat to boiling, ladle into sterilized jars, and then process for 10 minutes in a boiling water bath. Refer to "Boiling Water Bath" on page 18 for detailed processing instructions.

Pectin Portion

High-pectin Fruits: Apples (sour); cherries (sour); crabapples; cranberries; black, white, and red currants; gooseberries; grapefruit; Eastern Concord, Muscadine, and Scuppernog grapes; kiwifruit; lemons; limes; sour oranges; Damson and other tart plums; quince

Medium-pectin Fruits: Apples (sweet); apricots; blackberries; blueberries; boysenberries; loganberries; raspberries; tayberries

Low-pectin Fruits: Bananas; cherries (sweet); elderberries; figs; grapes (except varieties listed above); melons; nectarines; peaches; pears; pineapple; pomegranates; rhubarb; strawberries; sweet and Italian plums

Acids

Acid is the final part of the trinity that, along with sugar and pectin, improves flavor and combats growth of microorganisms in home-canned goods. Achieving the proper amount of acid is imperative in order to safely process items in a boiling water bath. Furthermore, acid helps jams, jellies, and preserves to gel properly while keeping pickles crispy. It also adds characteristic zip to relishes and salsas. The type of item you are preparing determines which variety of acid you will use.

Vinegar

Often used in pickling, a dash or two of vinegar can also be added to jams and jellies for unexpected flavor. Use only commercially prepared vinegars that can guarantee a consistent level of acidity. When vinegar is used as an acidifying agent, it must contain at least five percent acetic acid, also known as "50-grain." Homemade vinegars have unknown acidity levels, presenting possible health risks if used in the home canning of low-acid foods processed in a boiling water bath.

A medley of vinegars

Stay on the safe side and look for vinegars at your local grocer with labels reading "5% acidity" or higher. Apple cider vinegar and distilled white vinegar are recommended, as their acidity levels are usually right on target, but they are by no means the only options available. Balsamic, red and white wine, sherry, and many flavored vinegars may also be suitable; simply check the label to determine if the acidity label makes it safe for use.

If you have difficulty finding flavored vinegars with acidity levels at five percent or higher, start with a mild-flavored vinegar, such as distilled white or white wine, and infuse it for two to three weeks with whole spices. Strain out the spice at the end of the infusing period. Cloves, black pepper, cumin, fennel, juniper, cardamom...the options for homemade flavored vinegars are limited only by your imagination. Try adding your infused vinegar to pickles, relishes, and chutneys for extra pep.

Lemon Juice

Lemon juice is often the acid of choice when making jams, jellies, marmalades, and conserves. Or

Lemon juice and citric acid

bottled lemon juice should be used, as its acidity level is more consistent than that of fresh juice. Just like other fruits, the acidity level of lemon juice can vary from one lemon to the next. Stick with the yellow bottle and definitely never use fresh lemon juice for low-acid items such as tomatoes or figs if you intend to process them in a boiling water bath.

Citric Acid

Citric acid is a powdered substance made from citrus fruit. It has a strong sour taste, so it's better used as an acidifying agent for tomatoes than for fruit spreads. To use citric acid in place of lemon juice, use $1/4$ teaspoon per pint and $1/2$ teaspoon per quart of tomatoes. Citric acid is commonly available at drugstores and natural foods stores.

Salt

It is entirely optional to use salt in many home-canned items. It serves no function in preservation for jams, jellies, chutneys, marmalades, conserves, butters, or curds. It is, however, essential in relishes, pickles, salsas, fermented foods like sauerkraut, and

Using the right kind of salt is essential.

noked foods, where it contributes to both flavor and texture, nce salt draws out moisture. When a canning recipe calls for alt, be sure to use only salts labeled "canning," "pickling," or :osher." Never use table salt, as it is likely to contain anticak- ง agents that will turn the brining water cloudy. Table salt sually contains iodine, as well, which can darken your canned ่ods. Salts specifically indicated for home-canning use are ่ee of iodine and anticaking additives and are very fine- ่rained, making them dissolve easily.

lerbs and Spices

/hen using herbs and spices in your home-canned goods, ่esh is always best. The flavor and aroma produced by fresh asil or just-ground cardamom simply dwarfs that produced by ่eir dried and preground cousins. Buy spices in small quanti- ่es as often as needed to ensure freshness. Many natural food ่ores sell herbs and spices in the bulk section, which is a fan- ่stic way to save money, as purchasing entire jars can quickly ่dd up. Simply scoop out the amount you need, label your bag, ่nd use your supply without delay. If you are pickling, stick to ่hole spices, as adding them ground will cloud the brining ่olution. Spices added to jams, jellies, chutneys, marmalades,

conserves, or butters are better in their whole form, as well. Make a spice bundle out of cheesecloth or a muslin drawstring tea bag, and let it infuse the mixture as you cook. Remove the bundle from your finished batch before filling jars.

When using herbs, the volatile oils present in the plant's tis- sues are released as soon as they are broken, making both the taste and fragrance of dried herbs nowhere near as robust as that of those just harvested. Packaged fresh herbs can get costly rather quickly. If you anticipate you'll be using a lot of herbs, consider growing your own. You don't even need a yard to enjoy fresh tar- ragon, thyme, or rosemary. Got a sunny windowsill? That's really pretty much all you'll need in order to successfully grow fresh herbs all through the winter, spring, summer, or fall. If you are an experienced gardener, start your herbs from seed. Otherwise, keep an eye out at garden stores, nurseries, farmers' markets, or grocery stores for potted herbs.

Any herb or spice works well in home canning. Don't limit yourself to old standbys like mustard seed and chili flakes. In my kitchen, I love big, bold, unexpected culinary elements. For herbs consider lemon verbena, rosemary, dill, tarragon, thyme (of which there are many varieties worth sampling), geranium, lavender, mint, lemongrass, marjoram, and basil. Spices I adore include star anise, fennel seed, coriander, cumin, celery seed, nutmeg, ginger, cinnamon, juniper berries, all- spice, whole cloves, and peppercorns.

Prep School

Some ingredients will need to be prepped in advance of cooking. Reading through a recipe in advance will give you a heads-up on preliminary steps to be dealt with before starting a recipe. While most food prep in home canning is fairly straightforward, there are two techniques meriting a bit of elaboration: washing and blanching.

Washing

When cleaning produce to be used in home canning, removing every last bit of dirt should be your top priority. Botulism

spores live in dirt and soil, so it is imperative that you get out all traces of dirt before preparing your recipe. Even if you don't see any soil on the surface of the produce items you will be using, it is still a good idea to give everything a good rinse and a thorough scrubbing with a vegetable brush just prior to use. For delicate items such as berries, simply rinsing well with cool water will loosen up any remaining debris.

Blanching

The skins of some produce items will need to be removed before they are ready for use in a recipe. Otherwise, the skin's texture can become chewy and rubbery after cooking, not at all what you want people to notice when enjoying your peach chutney at brunch or digging into the jar of tomato jam you gave them as thanks for pet sitting. Blanching is also used with some vegetables in order to keep their color vibrant once canned. Fortunately this cooking technique couldn't be easier. Follow these simple steps to remove skins or boost color.

Blanching Peaches, Plums, Onions, and Tomatoes

Wash your produce under cool water. Prepare an ice bath by filling a large bowl with cold water and ice and setting it in the sink. Fill a medium stainless-steel pot two-thirds full with water. Bring to boil over high heat. Using a slotted spoon, gently place one item at a time into the boiling water. Boil for 30 seconds, remove the item with a slotted spoon, and immediately plunge it into the ice bath. Continue until each item has been blanched. The skins should slip off easily.

Prepare your ice bath in advance.

Blanching Vegetables for Color

The items most suited to blanching for color retention are listed below, accompanied by blanching times. Follow the instructions above for removing skins, substituting blanching times as appropriate.

Asparagus: 2 minutes

Beans (green and wax): 2 to 3 minutes

Beets: 20 minutes

Broccoli: 2 minutes

Brussels sprouts: 3 minutes

Carrots: 2 minutes

Cauliflower: 3 minutes

Corn (cut): 4 minutes

Okra: 3 minutes

Onions: 1½ minutes

Peas: 1½ minutes

Portrait of a canner

Walter

Walter, a sustainable farmer, learned his way around a boiling water bath a long time ago. Two generations ago, to be specific. He now runs a seventh-generation family-owned farm, using his grandmother's recipes to produce apple butter and blueberry, blackberry, and raspberry jam. When asked his motivation for putting up preserves, Walter mentions how canning "extends our marketing season beyond what is available for fresh fruit."

Every time he cans, Walter and his wife Wendy produce 500 jars of fruity goodness. They've been doing this for over 10 years, and their efforts are paying off. Although Walter's farm is situated in a rural spot tucked into the Appalachian Mountains, his products have far-reaching sales. A highly visible presence at a popular farmers' market, coupled with sales to area restaurants, natural foods stores, and Internet traffic, help make his Imladris Farm jams and butters successful. Passing on a bit of seasoned home canning wisdom to those just starting out, Walter jokingly cautions that "strawberry jam foams. A lot. No, really, a whole lot." Consider yourself forewarned by someone well steeped in the trade.

GIFT BASKETS

Gift baskets can be a tasteful and welcome way to share your handcrafted wares. Consider your recipient's interests and palate, if you know it, and build your theme from there. Don't limit yourself to old-school Easter baskets either. Square, rectangular, and oval shapes work just as well and may offer greater opportunities for continued use after your goodies have been gobbled up. Here's a smattering of ideas to borrow inspiration from.

High Tea: Fill the basket with a variety of curds, butters, jams, and marmalades. A scone mix and box of Earl Grey tea will drive the theme home.

Citrus Zest: Lemon curd, orange marmalade, preserved lemons, and candied kumquats combine for a basket that would work equally well for grandma in Florida or for a friend suffering from winter doldrums.

A Peck of Pickled Peppers: For those who like to feel the heat, combine habanero jelly, pickled jalapeños, and pickled sweet peppers.

Slow Jams: For the foodie in your life, try four seasons of jam with pear, cranberry, strawberry, and peach.

Visions of Sugarplums: Put together a holiday-themed basket for the family member or neighbor who really tricks out their house every December. Jars of pear and ginger mincemeat, 3-citrus marmalade, and apple and cranberry chutney will help make the holidays even brighter!

Community Supported Agriculture (CSA)

Community Supported Agriculture is a means for individuals to contribute resources and labor to ensure a farm's continued success. CSA members buy annual shares, enabling the farmer to purchase materials, grow the crops, and have a guaranteed market. Members in turn are assured a weekly box of locally grown produce and, in some instances, eggs and meat products. Members can make requests that certain items be planted at the beginning of a growing season and are frequently encouraged to come out and perform tasks on the farm itself, although contributing labor is optional in most cases. CSAs create a form of community farming, with all members, including the farmer, sharing in the risks and rewards that living off the land can entail. This model of farming began in Europe and Japan during the 1960s as a response to concerns over food safety and the loss of available farmland. Though the term "CSA" is used primarily by U.S. farms, there are similar farming models in existence worldwide. Check www.LocalHarvest.org for CSA farms in the United States, or search the internet for international CSA farms.

BIODYNAMIC FARMING

Biodynamics is a form of organic agriculture, developed by Austrian philosopher, educator, and social thinker Rudolf Steiner, that regards farms as discrete entities, composed of individual and collective organisms working in concert. In the biodynamic approach, the goal is achieving balance between soil organisms, plant matter, and animals in a symbiotic, closed, self-sustaining system. A form of organic farming, Biodynamics eschews the use of toxic pesticides and artificial fertilizers. Fermented herbal and mineral mixtures obtained from materials available on the farm itself are applied to compost materials and crops. Furthermore, soil preparation, planting, and harvest are done according to an astrological calendar that designates certain days as more or less conducive to plant vitality. Biodynamic production methods are employed all over the world. If a product you are consuming has "Demeter" on it, then you've got a biodynamic item on your hands.

Chapter 5

A Jams, Jellies, and Preserves Primer

I can think of few culinary experiences more transcendent, more deeply palate pleasing, than jam on toast. Crispy, crackly, almost caramelized toast, smothered i fragrant, tart-sweet strawberry jam or spicy apple but paired with a warm mug of tea or fresh glass of juice— there anything better? Jams, jellies, and preserves hav a way of bringing us back to childhood, when peanut better and jelly sandwiches ruled the lunchbox and ja left its sticky traces on faces and hands.

Jams, jellies, and preserves can be as sophisticated as simple as you like. Beginning with fruit, sugar, and, on occasion, added pectin, these condiments are sub-lime when pared down to showcase the fruit, or glori-ous when made complex and heady with spices, herb and flavorings. Their versatility has established them staples in all kitchens. Any way you stir the pot, these condiments never fail to tickle the taste buds.

WHAT'S IN A NAME?

Jams, jellies, preserves, conserves, marmalades, fruit butters, and fruit curds are close kin. All contain a mixture of fruit and sugar that is cooked until thickened. What distinguishes these fruit concoctions from one another is the type of fruit used, the size of the fruit pieces, the addition or omission of flavoring ingredients, and the manner in which the fruit and sugar mixture is processed. Let's examine each.

Jam A cooked mixture of fruit and sugar, in jam the fruit is finely chopped, mashed, or crushed. Jams should hold up firmly, but still be spreadable. When fruit is cooked only with fruit juices and no added sugar, the resulting mixture is sometimes called a "fruit spread" instead of a jam.

Jelly Jelly is a cooked mixture of fruit and sugar that is strained, resulting in a clear spread. Jellies should be completely solid and easy to cut and spread with a knife. To make jelly, strain cooked fruit through a mesh fabric bag (known as a jelly bag) or cheesecloth-lined sieve that is suspended over a bowl. Once the liquids have drained out, they are returned to the stovetop and cooked with sugar until a gel is formed.

Preserves A cooked mixture of fruit and sugar, preserves are made from fruit left in large pieces or chunks. Aside from the size of the fruit bits, preserves are otherwise very much akin to jams. To be considered a preserve, the fruits mustn't be crushed, minced, chopped, mashed, or cut into small bits. Small whole fruits, especially berries, or larger fruits cut into big chunks, are used in preserve making.

Conserves This spread is a cooked mixture of fruit, sugar, nuts, raisins, and often, dried fruits and spices. Conserves are similar in texture to jam, where the fruit is cut finely, mashed, or crushed, and then cooked. Most conserves contain more than one fruit and contain some sort of citrus.

Marmalade Marmalade is a cooked mixture of fruit (most commonly citrus) and sugar that is somewhere between jam and jelly in consistency. Pieces of lemon, orange, tangerine, lime, or grapefruit peel are suspended in a jelly-like base. Most recipes will direct you that the pith be completely removed from citrus peels prior to cooking, otherwise a bitter taste will be imparted. If you enjoy a bitter flavor, as I do, you need not be as fastidious about removing the pith when making marmalade to your own taste.

Fruit Butters Fruit butters are a fruit and sugar mixture where cooked fruit such as apple or pear is pureed and then combined with sugar and heated until smooth and velvety. The resulting spread should be thick and contain no runny juices. Cooking times for butters are highly variable, depending in large part on the juiciness of your fruit.

Curds Fruit curds are a mixture of citrus fruit, sugar, butter, and eggs, cooked to a smooth, thick, puddinglike texture. As curds contain eggs, they require either refrigeration (where they will keep for about 4 weeks) or pressure canning. If you opt to pressure can, try to eat, or gift, your curds within 3 to 4 months, as the flavor diminishes over time. In my experience, consuming curds in a timely manner has never been an issue.

Jam

Jelly

Preserve

Conserve

Marmalade

Fruit Butter

Curds

Troubleshooting Tips

If you follow the directions in this book and practice safe and hygienic home canning practices, the likelihood of mishaps will be considerably reduced. Nevertheless, snafus may occur. Learning what caused your seal to fail or your jelly to refuse to set will hopefully help prevent repeat performances the next time you decide to whip up some sweet spreads.

If your spread won't set:

◻ You may have used either too much or too little sugar. Follow recipes exactly as written, as adjusting the sugar content can negatively affect the spread's ability to gel.

◻ You may have had insufficient pectin, or the commercial pectin you used may have expired. Use the amount indicated in a recipe. If your pectin was coming from the fruit itself, you may need to add some supplemental pectin to create a gel.

◻ You may have used fruit that was overripe. Always choose fruits that are just at the peak of ripeness, but not past. Plan your canning for days when you will either be purchasing ripe fruit or harvesting fruit that is at peak ripeness.

◻ You may have not provided enough acid for a gel to occur. Add supplemental acid in the form of lemon juice.

◻ You may have cooked your mixture for too long after commercial pectin was added, or for too long after the intrinsic pectin in the fruit was released. Boil your mixture for only as long as indicated in the recipe.

◻ You may be dealing with a jelly that takes time to set up; be aware that some jellies set over time, needing as much as 2 weeks to firm.

If your spread is too tough:

◻ You may have overcooked your mixture, causing too much liquid to evaporate. Cook your mixture for only the amount of time indicated in the recipe.

◻ You may have used underripe fruit. Always choose fruits that are just at the peak of ripeness.

◻ You may have provided either too little sugar or too much acid. Follow the measurements in the recipe exactly.

If your jelly becomes cloudy:

◻ You may have used underripe fruit and the starch present in it caused the juice to cloud. Always use fruits that are just at the peak of ripeness.

◻ You may have squeezed the jelly bag or cheesecloth while it was dripping. Tempting as it may be, don't squeeze your extractor, as doing so can cloud the juice.

◻ You may have allowed your jelly to cool a bit in the pan before pouring it into the jars. Have all jars and lids ready and your boiling water bath prepared so that you can pour the mixture into jars as soon as it is done cooking.

If your spread darkens:

◻ You may have overcooked your mixture. Always follow cooking times as written in the recipe.

◻ You may have stored your preserves in too bright a location. Keep your canned goods in a dark spot after processing, such a pantry, cupboard, or basement.

◻ You may have stored your preserves in too warm a location. Keep your canned goods in a cool location, ideally between 40° to 70°F (4–21°C).

If your spread has mold or mildew:

◻ You may have failed to process your jars properly in a boiling water bath after cooking. Always process for the amount of time indicated (remember to adjust for altitude), and only begin timing after water is at a full, rolling, and sustained boil.

◻ You may have failed to provide adequate sugar or acid. Always measure ingredients as indicated in the recipe.

◻ You may have stored your preserves in too warm a location. Keep your canned goods in a cool spot, ideally between 40°F to 70°F (4–21°C).

If your spread has crystals:

◻ You may have failed to dissolve the sugar completely before bringing the mixture to a boil. Always allow the sugar to completely dissolve in the fruit juice or water over low heat before bringing to a full boil.

◻ You may have added too much sugar. Measure out and use only the amount of sugar indicated in the recipe.

◻ You may have insufficient acid in your mixture. Add supplementary lemon juice until the crystals dissolve.

Portrait of a canner

Donna

"No one is ever too young to learn to cook or can." Or so goes the canning wisdom of Donna. Currently spending her time as a homemaker and caretaker, Donna's entire extended family has been engaged in home canning in some fashion or other for as long as she can remember. Her grandfather, Ralph, would gather up the kids each summer and head to a nearby peach farm to pick the heady fruit in abundance, often returning home with as many as 20 bushels. It was then the task of her grandmother, Ora, to jar those sunny orbs, preserving the tender flesh and sweet promise of summertime so that they might be enjoyed year-round. Donna also recalls family-wide hog butchering events. Everyone would participate, creating sausage that would then be canned, as doing so extends the shelf life far longer than freezing alone.

It was from Ora that Donna learned the ropes of food preservation. She continues to learn new techniques, recently adding a friend's prized bread-and-butter pickles recipe to her repertoire. Home canning is an annual occurrence in Donna's home, where she puts up everything from tomatoes to pickles, from green beans to soup mixes. She also cooks up batches of jams and jellies, as well as homemade blackberry wine from her own berries and apple butter from a neighbor's trees. For Donna, it's all about freshness and flavor. "Grocery stores are a convenience, but there is nothing better than home-grown or homemade food."

DONNA'S BITS O' CANNING WISDOM

- "Can because you enjoy it...never make it a job or task."
- "Keep your food preparation area clean, and always sterilize your jars well."
- "Grandmother always told me to remove the rings from my jars when storing; if anything spoils, the lids will come off. Food that is good holds its seal."

Portrait of a canner

Lisa

A self-described "organic vegetable farmer/poet/herbalist/enrichment teaching assistant," Lisa, along with her husband, Mark, and two grown children, steward the land at Mountain Dell Farm in upstate New York. In addition to growing produce destined for restaurants in New York City, the family supplies nearby natural food stores, restaurants, and individuals, as well as running a small CSA (Community Supported Agriculture).

With so much time spent toiling the soil, you'd think Lisa would have little time left for home canning. Yet she manages to pull it off, and has done so for 20 years! She cans between five and 10 times annually, depending on what is available. In her kitchen you'll find everything from dilly beans, elderberry jelly and juice, black and red currant jellies, raspberry jelly, applesauce, pear and apple butters, pickled beets, salsa, and tomatoes to lacto-fermented daikon pickles, cucumber pickles, and kimchee.

Canning is an act of necessity for Lisa and her family, producing benefits on a number of fronts. The technique provides a means of dealing with "an abundance of fresh produce. It tastes good, is healthy, and saves money. It's the only way you can eat certain foods."

Strawberry Jam

trawberry jam is pretty much the rock star of the jam
rld. Everyone seems to like it, it's easy to make, and you
t an incredible return for rather little effort. The only
vance preparation required in this recipe (short of prep-
g the fruit) involves allowing the strawberries, sugar, and
non juice to sit together for 2 hours before cooking. This
ses the natural juices of the strawberries to be released,
ich in turn helps the pectin in the berries to be more
ailable when you begin cooking. *Yield: 3 half pints*

> 4   pints strawberries, hulled
>   and sliced
>
> 2   cups granulated sugar
>
> 2   tablespoons bottled
>   lemon juice

Skimming foam from the surface *bottom:* **Test for gelling.**

TO PREPARE:

1. Place two small plates in the freezer. These will be used later to test for gelling.

2. In a large nonmetallic bowl, add the strawberries, sugar, and lemon juice; stir, cover loosely with a kitchen cloth, and set aside to macerate at room temperature for 2 hours.

3. Sterilize three half-pint mason jars, lids, and screw rings (refer to page 29 for detailed instructions). Fill a canner or large stockpot with water, and set over medium-high heat. Bring just to the boiling point. Place the lids in a small saucepan, fill with water, bring to a boil, turn off the heat, and set the pan aside.

4. Transfer the strawberry mixture to a medium stainless-steel pot. Bring to a boil over medium-high heat and boil for 20 to 25 minutes, until the mixture begins to thicken. Stir frequently and watch the pot carefully to prevent the contents from boiling over. Skim off any foam that rises to the top.

5. Test for gelling. Remove a plate from the freezer and spoon about 1 teaspoon of the strawberry mixture onto it. Place the plate back in the freezer and wait 2 minutes. Remove from the freezer and push the edge of the jam with your fingertip. If the jam has gelled properly, the surface will wrinkle a bit. If it fails to wrinkle, or is obviously still runny, boil the jam for 5 minutes longer, and then repeat the test.

6. Place the hot, sterilized jars on top of a kitchen cloth on the counter. With the help of a canning funnel, ladle jam into the jars, reserving 1/4-inch (6 mm) headspace. Use a nonmetallic spatula to remove any trapped air bubbles, and wipe the rims clean with a damp cloth. Place on the lids and screw bands, tightening only until fingertip-tight.

7. Using a jar lifter, place the jars into the canner. Process for 10 minutes in a boiling water bath (refer to page 32 for detailed instructions). Remember to adjust for altitude.
Variation: If you'd like to give your strawberry jam an herbal undertone reminiscent of summer, add 1 tablespoon fresh mint or lemon verbena. If fresh herbs aren't available, use 2 teaspoons dried.

Apple Butter

Apple butter invokes the most ideal elements of a crisp autumn day. You can almost smell piles of leaves being burned, feel the heat from steaming mugs of cider, and see resplendent foliage in fiery shades of orange, yellow, and red. This recipe makes an incredibly fragrant mixture with a rich, velvety texture. Your kitchen will smell amazing, and, if you're anything like me, you'll feel as though you are truly embracing the full splendor of the autumn season. Cooking apples work best; good choices include Golden Delicious, Granny Smith, Gravenstein, McIntosh, Newton, Pippin, or Winesap. *Yield: 4 half-pints*

YOU WILL NEED:

- 5 pounds cooking apples
- 2 cups granulated sugar
- 2 teaspoons ground cinnamon
- ½ teaspoon ground cloves
- ½ teaspoon ground nutmeg
- ½ teaspoon ground ginger

An apple peeler is quite the time saver.

TO PREPARE:

1. Peel, core, and roughly chop the apples. Place in a large stainless-steel pot along with 2 cups water. Simmer over low heat for 45 minutes. Stir occasionally to prevent sticking, and add water in ¼ cup increments if sticking occurs. Remove from heat.

2. Press the cooked apple mixture through a food mill or fine-meshed sieve, purée in a food processor once slightly cooled, or use an immersion blender and purée the mixture in the pot.

3. Return the apple purée to the pot, add the sugar and spices, and bring to a gentle boil over medium heat. Reduce the heat to low, and simmer for 25 to 30 minutes. Stir often to prevent sticking. Remove from heat.

4. While the apple butter cooks, sterilize four half-pint mason jars, lids, and screw rings (refer to page 29 for detailed instructions). Fill a canner or large stockpot with water, and set over medium-high heat. Bring just to the boiling point. Place the lids in a small saucepan, fill with water, bring to a boil, turn off the heat, and set the pan aside.

5. Place the hot jars on top of a kitchen cloth on the counter. With the help of a canning funnel, ladle apple butter into the jars, reserving ¼-inch (6 mm) headspace. Use a nonmetallic spatula to remove any trapped air bubbles, and wipe the rims clean with a damp cloth. Place on the lids and screw bands, tightening only until fingertip-tight.

6. Using a jar lifter, place the jars into the canner. Process for 10 minutes in a boiling water bath (refer to page 32 for detailed instructions). Remember to adjust for altitude. **Variation:** Use only cinnamon, or omit the spices altogether, for a basic apple butter where the flavor of the apples shines through.

Grape Jelly

A perennial favorite of children and adults alike (not to mention budget-wise college students), grape jelly is the perfect solution for tempering the innate tartness of grapes. Spread heavily over peanut butter, grape jelly aids in producing what is arguably the ultimate quick and tasty sandwich. It also pairs flawlessly when matched with a spicy chili sauce and poured over meatballs, producing a robust appetizer. Of course, it's also quite good straight out of the jar, thank you very much! *Yield: 4 half-pints*

TO PREPARE:

1. Rinse grapes under cool water. Remove from stems and place in a medium stainless-steel pot. Don't bother removing the seeds, if present, as they will be strained out later in the jelly bag or cheesecloth. Add ¾ cup water, crush grapes lightly with a wooden spoon or mallet, and place over high heat. Bring to a boil, reduce heat, cover, and simmer 12 minutes, stirring frequently to prevent scorching. Remove from heat.

2. Pour the grape mixture into either a moistened jelly bag or a strainer lined with several layers of cheesecloth. Place over a large bowl, and allow juice to drip out overnight or for a minimum of 2 hours.

3. Place two small plates in the freezer (these will be used later to test for gelling).

4. Sterilize 4 half-pint mason jars, lids, and screw rings (refer to page 29 for detailed instructions). Fill a canner or large stockpot with water, and set over medium-high heat. Bring just to boiling point. Place lids in a small saucepan, fill with water, bring to a boil, turn off heat, remove from the stovetop, and set aside.

5. Mix ¼ cup sugar with pectin in a small bowl. Transfer the collected grape juice to a medium stainless-steel pot, add sugar-pectin mixture, and bring to a boil over medium-high heat. Once juice has reached a full boil, add additional sugar, and boil rapidly for 2 minutes. Skim off any foam that rises to the top of the boiling mixture.

6. Test for gelling. Remove a plate from the freezer and spoon about 1 teaspoon of the grape mixture onto it. Place back in the freezer and wait 2 minutes. Remove the plate from the freezer and push the edge of the jelly with your fingertip. If it has gelled properly, the surface will wrinkle a bit. If it fails to wrinkle, or is obviously still runny, continue cooking the jelly for 2 minutes longer, and then repeat the test.

7. Place the hot jars on top of a kitchen cloth on the counter. With the help of a canning funnel, ladle jelly into the jars, reserving ¼-inch (6 mm) headspace. Use a nonmetallic spatula to remove any trapped air bubbles, and wipe rims clean with a damp cloth. Place on lids and screw bands, tightening only until fingertip-tight.

8. Using a jar lifter, place the jars into the canner. Process for 10 minutes in a boiling water bath (refer to page 32 for detailed instructions). Remember to adjust for altitude.

Variation: To impart a bit of unexpected herbal vigor to your jelly, consider adding herbes de Provence. Named after the sunny region in southern France, the herbal blend consists of varying amounts of bay leaf, thyme, fennel, rosemary, chervil, oregano, summer savory, tarragon, mint, marjoram, and lavender. Place 1 tablespoon dried herbes de Provence in a muslin pouch, secure at the top, and add to the grape mixture after the sugar has dissolved. Remove once the mixture begins to gel, and process as above.

Chapter 6

A Pickle, Relish, and Chutney Primer

Pickles, along with relishes and chutneys, help appetizers, salads, and entrees become more fully energized, enlivened, and complete. These condiments add twang and puckery perfection to the fruits and vegetables they are preserved alongside. The common element connecting pickles, relishes and chutneys is that they are all preserved in an acid solution, most commonly based on vinegar.

PICKLES

Pickles are commonly processed in one of two ways: fermented or fresh pack. While the cucumber is pickling's star, everything from okra to watermelon rind to pears can be pickled. Fresh-pack and fermented pickles are markedly distinct entities. If you are unsure whether you've actually had a "pickled" pickle, you most likely haven't. Once you have, you'll know. The flavor and aroma of fermented pickles is distinctly sour and pungent. While it can overwhelm delicate nasal passages, I find it intoxicating.

To create fermented pickles, also called crock or barrel pickles, vegetables or fruits are covered in a brine. Pickling brine is simply a solution of water, salt, vinegar, and varying herbs and spices. The brine-covered mixture is then left to cure at around 70°F (21°C) for 2 to 6 weeks. During this time, the atmospheric conditions inside the container will allow bacteria to produce lactic acid. It is this lactic acid

that serves to preserve the vegetables or fruits, keeping them from rotting and imbuing them with their characteristic "pickley" essence. Many enthusiasts rave about the benefits of lactic acid, including improved digestion. I won't be offering any fermented pickle recipes in this book, as a proper discussion of fermentation truly merits an entire book of its own. I do suggest further exploration for those who are curious. The website of the National Center for Home Food Preservation is a wonderful resource on fermentation: http://uga.edu/nchfp.

If you don't have the patience to wait for fermented pickles, fresh pack may be the best pickling method for you. Fresh pack also involves creating a brine. This brine is then poured over fresh vegetables or fruits packed in canning jars, after which the jars are processed in a boiling water bath. You'll find a recipe for fresh-packed dill pickles on page 72.

Fermented pickles (right) show a cloudy brine.

RELISHES

Relishes are similar to pickles in their use of acid to preserve foods. What distinguishes both relishes and chutneys from pickles is that ingredients are chopped and cooked before they are jarred. Relishes can be sweet, spicy, savory, or all three. While the first relish you might think of is the sweet, bright green pickle relish of hot dog fame, many other relishes exist. I'll share with you savory alternatives in my recipes for Fennel Relish (page 102) and Beet and Sage Relish (page 125). Relishes aren't limited to vegetables, either. Fabulous condiments can be made from many fruits, including pineapples, apricots, and cranberries.

CHUTNEYS

Chutneys tend to be primarily fruit-based, although vegetable-based recipes are not unheard of. This condiment is characterized by its spiciness, ranging from the mild heat produced by ginger to the fiery blaze of cayenne and chili peppers. Chutneys tend to be saucier than relishes; some are smooth while others are chunky. Although most commonly associated with Indian foods, chutney can highlight the flavors of any cuisine. Spread on a sandwich, served alongside cheese and pickles, or paired with a pork loin, chutney instantly adds zip and interest. In this book, we'll explore a year's worth of seasonal chutneys, from Curried Winter Squash Chutney (page 100) to Rhubarb and Amaretto Chutney (page 108).

Troubleshooting Tips

Sometimes, things just don't turn out right when making pickles, relishes, and chutneys, even for experienced home canners. The pickles get mushy, the color is off, the brine turns cloudy—the pickles are just not cooperating. Knowing in advance what to be aware of during prep and processing can help limit mishaps. The following pickle problems are those most frequently encountered in home pickle making. With relishes and chutneys, I've found that if you stick to the recipe, few things go wrong. Do make sure to always follow suggestions for headspace. If you fill your jar too full, it's likely to overflow during processing.

If your pickles are soft:

☐ You might have added too little salt or vinegar with low acidity. Be sure to use commercial vinegars with 5 to 7 percent acid; it will be marked on the bottle as such.

☐ You might have left the blossom end on the cucumbers. These must be removed before processing, as an enzyme in them can make pickles soft once jarred.

☐ You may have left the pickles in too warm an environment. The ideal temperature for storing fermented pickles is between 70° and 75°F (21° and 24°C).

If your pickles are hollow:

☐ You might have used cucumbers too long off the vine before pickling. Ideally, pickling cucumbers should be harvested no more than 48 hours before processing, with 24 hours being ideal. To test whether your cucumbers are hollow, put them in a bowl and cover with cold water. If they float, use them for relish, instead. Sinkers should be fine for pickling whole.

☐ You might have made your brine either too strong or too weak for fermentation to occur. Follow your recipe expressly as indicated, and be sure to use vinegar with 5 to 7 percent acidity.

If your pickles are tough:

☐ You might have used too much salt. Carefully measure all salt to be used in recipes; "winging it" can sometimes result in too little or too much.

☐ You might have processed your pickles too long. Set a timer so that you only process as long as necessary.

☐ You might have used cucumbers harvested some time before pickling. Ideally, pickling cucumbers should be harvested no more than 48 hours before processing, with 24 hours being ideal.

If your pickles are dark:

☐ You might have used ground spices in the brine. When pickling, it's best to use whole spices.

☐ You might have used table salt. Only use pickling or kosher salt in pickling, as anticaking agents in table salt can cause an off color.

☐ You may have hard water containing iron or other metals. Use either soft or distilled water.

If your pickles are moldy:

☐ Your fruits or vegetables might not have been washed thoroughly before processing. Give every item you intend to pickle a thorough wash and scrub before use.

☐ You might have used cucumbers harvested some time before pickling. Ideally, pickling cucumbers should be harvested no more than 48 hours before processing, with 24 hours being ideal.

If your brine is cloudy:

☐ You might be witnessing the presence of lactic acid. If you are making fermented pickles, cloudiness indicates that the lactic acid is doing its thing.

☐ You might have spoiled pickles. If you are making fresh-pack pickles, cloudiness could indicate the presence of bacteria. Check for stinky smells or mushy texture. If neither is present, your pickles are safe to eat. Otherwise, toss them into the compost.

☐ You might have used table salt. Use only pickling or kosher salt in pickling, as anticaking agents in table salt can cause an off color.

☐ You may have hard water containing iron or other metals. Use either soft or distilled water.

Basic, All-Purpose Brine for Picklin

This delicious and easy three-step pickle recipe can be used for a wide range of summer's bounty. The formula is three parts vinegar to one part water; the amount of sugar and salt can vary according to taste. Anything that's crisp and fresh can be put up in this well-balanced solution. Favorites are okra; green or yellow wax beans; carrots; cherry peppers; small onions; cauliflower; baby summer squash such as zucchini, yellow, or pattypan; and, of course, cucumbers. Adjust or change seasonings according to your taste or desired spiciness. This recipe makes enough pickling liquid to fill approximately 4 pints of packed jars. (Recipe graciously provided by Chris, who you can read more about in his profile on page 78.)

3 cups white vinegar

½ cup sugar (may use less, but don't omit entirely)

2 tablespoons pickling salt

Prepared horseradish

Peppercorns (may use a blend of black, white, and green)

Celery seed

Fresh dill or tarragon

Garlic cloves, peeled

Hot cayenne pepper (optional)

2. Sterilize 4 pint or 2 quart mason jars, lids, and screw rings (refer to page 29 for detailed instructions). Fill a canner or large stockpot with water, and set it over medium-high heat. Bring just to the boiling point. Place the lids in a small saucepan, fill with water, bring to a boil, turn off the heat, and set the pan aside.

3. Combine vinegar, 1 cup water, sugar, and salt in a small saucepan. Bring the brine to a boil. Reduce heat and hold at a simmer, covered, while packing your jars.

4. Place your hot jars on top of a kitchen towel on the counter. Into the bottom of each sterilized jar, add the following: ½ teaspoon horseradish, 6 peppercorns, ⅛ teaspoon celery seed, a sprig of dill or tarragon (or ¼ teaspoon dill seed; ⅛ teaspoon dried tarragon), 1 garlic clove, and 1 cayenne pepper (whole, halved, or quartered lengthwise).

5. Pack the vegetables tightly into the jars, and add hot pickling liquid. Slip a nonmetallic spatula down the side of each, and carefully tip the jar slightly to allow brine to fill any voids. Pack to ½-inch (1.3 cm) headspace. Wipe the rims clean with a damp cloth. Place on lids and screw bands, tightening only until fingertip-tight.

6. Using a jar lifter, place the jars in the canner. Process pints 10 minutes and quarts 15 minutes in a boiling water bath (refer to page 32 for detailed instructions). Remember to adjust for altitude.

TO PREPARE:

1. Wash, scrub, and chop whatever vegetables you will be using. Hard vegetables such as cauliflower, squash, carrots, and cherry peppers can be packed more tightly into jars if slightly softened beforehand. Simply pour boiling water over the vegetables and allow them to soften for 5 to 10 minutes, just until they are resilient, then rinse in very cold water.

Dill Pickles

For many, a sandwich just isn't a sandwich unless it's accompanied by a dill pickle. In my opinion, their pungent saltiness is the perfect lunchtime companion. Aside from an overnight soak, this canning classic is ready in no time. **Yield: 8 pints**

YOU WILL NEED:

6 pounds pickling cucumbers

¾ cup pickling salt (divided)

4 cups white vinegar

Garlic cloves, peeled

Dill seed

Fresh dill heads (if unavailable, use dried dill)

Black peppercorns

TO PREPARE:

1. Rinse the cucumbers in cold water. Scrub gently with a vegetable brush to loosen any hidden soil. Remove a thin slice from the blossom end of each cucumber (if you can't tell which end is the blossom end, just take a thin slice off of each end). Place the cucumbers in a nonreactive glass or ceramic bowl, add ½ cup pickling salt, cover with water, place a plate or towel over the top, and set in a cool place or the refrigerator overnight or for 8 hours.

2. Drain off the brine. Rinse the cucumbers thoroughly to remove salt residue. Set aside.

3. Sterilize 8 pint mason jars, lids, and screw rings (refer to page 29 for detailed instructions).

4. In a medium stainless-steel pan, combine vinegar, 3½ cups water, and ¼ cup pickling salt. Bring the brine to a boil, reduce heat, and simmer for 5 minutes. Remove from heat, and set aside.

5. Into each sterilized jar, place 1 garlic clove, ½ teaspoon dill seed, 1 dill head or ½ teaspoon dried dill, and 8 black peppercorns.

6. Pack cucumbers into each jar, and cover with the vinegar solution. Leave ½-inch (1.3 cm) headspace. Use a nonmetallic spatula to remove any trapped air bubbles, and wipe the rims clean with a damp cloth. Place on lids and screw bands, tightening only until fingertip-tight.

7. Process for 10 minutes in a boiling water bath (refer to page 32 for detailed instructions). Remember to adjust for altitude.

Removing the blossom end of the cucumber

Sweet Pickle Relish

Classic southern deviled eggs and hot dogs pretty much owe their very existence to sweet pickle relish. Add a tablespoon or two to potato salad, and it's instantly elevated to new culinary heights. Sweet pickle relish harmoniously marries sweet and sour tastes, each flavor balancing and tempering the other. There's a reason this union has endured the test of time—its puckery sweetness punctuates and embellishes every dish it is paired with. *Yield: 6 half-pints*

YOU WILL NEED:

- 4 medium cucumbers, peeled, seeded, and diced
- 2 1/2 cups sweet onion, diced
- 1 cup green pepper, diced
- 1 cup sweet red pepper, diced
- 1/4 cup pickling or kosher salt
- 3 cups granulated sugar
- 2 1/2 cups cider vinegar
- 1 1/2 tablespoons yellow mustard seed
- 1 1/2 tablespoons celery seed
- 1 teaspoon turmeric

TO PREPARE:

1. Combine the cucumbers, sweet onion, green and red peppers, and salt in a large bowl. Toss to combine, cover with a kitchen towel, and let stand in a cool area overnight or for at least four hours.

2. Drain and rinse the vegetables in a colander. Rinse several times, pressing the vegetables with the back of a wooden spoon to remove all liquid and salty residue. Set aside.

3. Sterilize 6 half-pint jars, lids, and screw rings (refer to page 29 for detailed instructions).

4. In a medium stainless-steel saucepan, combine the sugar, vinegar, mustard seed, celery seed, and turmeric. Add the vegetables, and bring the mixture to a boil. Reduce heat to low, and simmer for 15 minutes.

5. Pack relish into the jars, leaving 1/2-inch (1.3 cm) headspace. Use a nonmetallic spatula to remove any trapped air bubbles, and wipe the rims clean with a damp cloth. Place on lids and screw bands, tightening only until fingertip-tight.

6. Process for 10 minutes in a boiling water bath (refer to page 32 for detailed instructions). Remember to adjust for altitude.

Quick Persian Pickles

Enjoy the heady fragrance and spicy zip of cumin, fennel, black pepper, and other Persian spices in this easy pickle recipe. Served alongside a hummus sandwich, homemade falafel, or even your basic burger, these crunchy goodies might become your new favorite thing. *Yield: 2 quarts*

YOU WILL NEED:

- 3 pounds pickling cucumbers
- 2½ cups distilled white vinegar
- ¼ cup granulated sugar
- 2 tablespoons pickling or kosher salt
- 6 whole garlic cloves, peeled
- 1 tablespoon fennel seed
- 1 tablespoon cumin seed
- 1 tablespoon coriander seed
- 1 tablespoon mustard seed
- 2 teaspoons whole cloves
- 1 tablespoon black peppercorns

TO PREPARE:

1. Thoroughly clean whatever containers you will be using to store your quick pickles once refrigerated. You can use any ceramic or glass container with a lid. Avoid metal and plastic vessels, as they can impart an off flavor.

2. Wash and gently scrub your cucumbers to remove any dirt or debris. Cut about ¼ inch (6 mm) from each end. Cut each cucumber in half, and place in a large bowl.

3. Next, combine 2½ cups water with the vinegar, sugar, salt, garlic, and spices in a medium saucepan over medium-high heat. Bring the brine to a boil, then reduce heat to low and simmer for 5 minutes. Remove from heat and cool for 15 minutes.

4. Pour the brine over the cucumbers. Cover the bowl lightly with a cloth and allow to cool for one hour. Transfer the pickles to refrigerator-bound containers, cover with a lid, and refrigerate.

5. Your pickles will need at least 24 hours to absorb the flavors of the spices. For the zestiest, best-tasting results, wait for one week, at which point the flavor will be much more pronounced. Quick Persian Pickles will keep for four weeks in the refrigerator.

Quick Pickles

Perhaps what you have is a hankering, not a mission. Possibly you have merely a cuke or two, not a bushel, and you've got a pickle itch that must be promptly scratched. Well, look no further; your healing balm has been found. If you crave the puckery twang of a pickle but don't want the time commitment involved in boiling water bath processing, then a quick, or refrigerator, pickle is just the thing you're after. The process goes something like this: You stir up a brine, chop up your veggies, add them to the brine, and park the whole thing in the fridge. Pickled ecstasy is yours within a week. Your quick pickles will stay fresh for about 3 weeks thereafter. It really is that easy.

Portrait of a canner

Chris

While his legitimate profession may be art director at a book publishing company, come summertime, Chris might as well hang a shingle on his door announcing his new position as "Full-time Director of Home Canning Operations." Growing up in a canning household—make that canning community—he's no stranger to boiling pots and jiggling pressure canners. His father maintained a 2-acre garden, the outpouring of which he, along with his mother, sisters, and aunt, would pluck, shuck, cut, blanch, pickle, and pack. In college, he gathered up one of his mother's extra canners, once he'd secured a kitchen of his own, and started pickling. The momentum built from there.

A member of a nearby CSA (Community Supported Agriculture) farm, Chris and his partner, Skip, make plans all summer for activities other than canning that just don't seem to materialize, or at least not according to the schedule they initially imagine. "Overabundance at local tailgate markets sets off a primitive hoarding instinct," Chris relays. "We'll declare the *next* weekend to be spent camping or tubing in a cold creek. Saturday comes and a favorite tailgate farmer will have bushels of perfect red cherry peppers, then it's Sunday evening and we're admiring our new jars of pickled peppers." Farmers' market offerings, coupled with those he receives weekly from his CSA, leave him with plenty to eat, freeze, can, or pickle.

Canning for him, though, isn't simply a chore to be dealt with. Chris's enthusiasm for home-canned goods also stems in large part from a desire to support agriculture as a way of life. "My way to support our local farm community is to buy large quantities of produce to preserve." That commitment manifests in whole and crushed tomatoes, tomato sauce, spicy tomato juice (for fresh-from-the-garden Bloody Marys!), Dixie relish, ketchup, tomato preserves, and Thai chili-garlic sauce. Furthermore, Chris and Skip make their own NY deli-tasting barrel pickles, and, their most prized home-canning product, French pickles. Using cornichons grown for them by their CSA farmer, the duo have developed a heavenly pickle, brined with herbs, pearl onions, garlic, peppercorns, and wine vinegar over several days. He now can't imagine summer without putting up several jars and has generously allowed his recipe to be shared here.

CHRIS'S CANNING WISDOM

- Always prep extra jars and lids. Yields can vary according to the water content of the fruit or vegetable and how tightly they pack into jars. You might end up needing to fill a couple of extra jars.

- The canning process sometimes dictates its own timeline. Your kitchen isn't normal that day. You should have a meal plan that's simple and easy and have some snacks nearby.

Chris's French Pickles

Chris's French Pickles

Start the four-day process of making French Pickles by preparing the brining ingredients. You will need a nonreactive container (glass, crockery, plastic, or stainless steel) that is at least 3 to 4 inches (7.6 to 10.2 cm) deeper than the cucumbers. You will also need a loose-fitting lid; a cookie sheet will do. Early season cucumbers are best for this recipe; try to find the smallest, freshest possible. Fresh tarragon makes a real difference in the flavor, but dried may be substituted if you can't find any.

FOR BRINING YOU WILL NEED:

5 to 6	pounds cucumbers
2	cups whole pearl onions
4 to 5	cloves garlic
$2/3$	cup pickling salt, divided

TO PREPARE:

1. Shave or cut the blossom ends off the cucumbers. Leave small cucumbers whole; split larger ones lengthwise.

2. Drop the onions into boiling water for 1 to 2 minutes. Rinse them in cold water, drain, then slip off the skins, leaving a small nub of root to hold each onion together. Cover and refrigerate until needed.

3. Peel and halve the garlic.

4. To gauge how much water to use, place the cucumbers in the brining container, cover with cold water, then measure the water.

5. Return the cucumbers to the brining container, and add the garlic. Cover with boiling water. Leave the vessel uncovered overnight. After the first day, you will need to change the water every 24 hours.

6. The next day, drain the cucumbers. Add the onions and sprinkle with $1/3$ cup pickling salt. Cover with boiling water. Cover the vessel loosely with the lid, leaving a 1- to 2-inch (2.5 to 5 cm) gap for air.

7. On the third day, repeat the process: Drain the cucumbers. Sprinkle with $1/3$ cup pickling salt. Cover with boiling water. Cover loosely with the lid.

8. If you're not ready to pickle on the fourth day, you may refrigerate cucumbers in brine an additional day. At pickling time, drain the cucumbers. Pierce each through with a fork in 2 to 3 places, being careful not to split them.

FOR PICKLING YOU WILL NEED:

5	cups white wine vinegar, 6 percent acidity or higher
1	cup water
$1/3$	cup granulated sugar
1	teaspoon salt
1	tablespoon fresh tarragon, chopped, or $1\frac{1}{2}$ teaspoons dried tarragon
$1/2$	teaspoon ground black pepper

FOR PACKING EACH JAR YOU WILL NEED:

1	sprig tarragon or $1/4$ teaspoon dried tarragon
4 or 5	whole green peppercorns
2 or 3	whole white peppercorns
	Pinch of red pepper flakes or fresh hot pepper (optional)
1	clove garlic, split lengthwise
	Cucumbers and onions

9. Prepare your jars, lids, and rings as described on page

10. Bring the pickling ingredients to a boil, then turn to low simmer while you are packing the jars.

11. Add the herbs and spices from packing ingredients jars. Pack the cucumbers and onions snuggly into jars, leaving $1/2$-inch (1.3 cm) headspace. Cover with the hot pickling solution. Slide a nonmetallic spatula into the side of the jar and tip from side to side so that brine fills any gaps. Top off with brine to leave $1/2$-inch (1.3 cm) headspace.

12. Process 10 minutes in boiling water bath. Remember adjust for altitude.

Chapter 7

A Whole Fruit and Vegetables Primer

For many, the motivation for home canning comes from a very real need to preserve a bounty of produ Whether your bumper crop comes from your own v etable patch, an irresistible bounty at a nearby farm market, or a too-good-to-pass-up sale at the grocer store, it's easy to suddenly find yourself swimming green beans, tomatoes, peaches, or any number of fruits and vegetables. A wonderful way to make the deliciousness of these items available year-round is preserve them in simple syrup or water for vegetab

Fruit, owing to its high acidity, can be safely can in a boiling water bath. The pH of whole tomatoes tends to straddle the low/high-acid fence; they can also be processed in a boiling water bath so long a proper amount of lemon juice or citric acid is adde (see Acidifying Tomatoes, page 47). All other vegeta must be processed in a pressure canner unless sup mental acid is provided. If you'd love to put up som corn, green beans, or asparagus, you'll need to get yourself a pressure canner. Detailed instructions fo using a pressure canner can be found on page 34. sure to familiarize yourself with the specific instru tions accompanying your particular model, as well

FRUIT

From peaches to plums and beyond, putting up fruits in their whole form affords great versatility for fruit-inspired concoctions during the off-seasons. In addition to providing yourself and your family with a pantry full of provisions, preserved fruits are lovely items for gift-giving, whether the occasion is a house-warming get-together, a birthday, or simply a "thank you."

Preparation

Naturally high in acid, fruit does not require pressure canning and can be safely processed in a boiling water bath. Figs are perhaps the one exception to this, with a pH around 4.6. As such, they'll need a bit of supplemental acid for water bath canning. If processing figs whole, add 1 teaspoon lemon juice per jar for safety.

To prep items for processing, gently scrub them with a vegetable brush in a sink of cold water, taking care to not bruise the flesh or puncture the skin. You may need to change the rinsing water several times if a good amount of dirt and debris is coming off of the fruit. Only wash as much fruit as can be canned in a single batch, as exposing fruit to water causes deterioration. Prep and can the first batch, and then move on to the next batch.

Some fruit will also need to have its skin removed. For apples or pears, use a vegetable peeler or paring knife to

gently remove the skin. For peaches and apricots, blanch the fruit for easy removal of the skin (see page 52 for detailed instructions on blanching). Plums, grapes, and cherries need not be peeled, but do best if their skins are gently pricked with a needle or fork tine; this helps prevent the skins from bursting when subjected to the high temperatures of the boiling water bath.

Preventing Browning

Some light-colored fruit, such as apples, pears, peaches, and apricots, will brown once its flesh is cut and exposed to oxygen. While not affecting the taste or quality, this discoloration makes the fruit less appealing once canned. To prevent discoloration, soak your fruit in an anti-

TIP:

While simply placing your fruit and vegetables in a jar, ladling preserving liquid over them, and firing up the boiling water bath or pressure canner are all that's truly required to put up produce, adding a few special touches makes your labor of love that much more appealing. Whether you will be the sole recipient of your wares or you intend to gift friends and family with jars of home-canned peaches or green beans, the addition of herbs or spices goes a long way toward imparting flavor and making the contents especially lovely. Whole star anise, cloves, and cinnamon sticks are aromatic and striking in their unique forms, perfectly complementing most fruit. Fresh basil, dill, tarragon, thyme, or marjoram will enliven vegetables and provide a punch of color.

browning solution. Commercial solutions can be found wherever home canning equipment is sold. Alternatively, you can make your own version one of two ways: Dissolve 1 teaspoon powdered citric acid in 1 gallon of water, or crush up six 500 mg water-soluble vitamin C tablets and add to 1 gallon of water. Make the solution before you begin peeling, cutting, or blanching the fruit. Add the fruit pieces to the solution as you are prepping your batch for canning. Never leave fruit in the solution for longer than 20 minutes, as doing so can compromise flavor. Before processing, drain the liquid off in a colander and give the fruit a quick rinse. As long as you remember to drain and rinse the antibrowning solution, it won't impart any flavor to your fruit.

Canning Syrups

While it is certainly possible to can fruit using only water as your preserving liquid, your fruit will become soft and darken within a matter of months. If you plan to polish off your jars quickly, a shortened shelf life might not be a problem. If you hope to keep your canned fruit for some time, however, then sugar syrup or fruit juice should be your canning liquid of choice. The inclusion of sugar helps fruit retain texture, shape, and color. Homemade sugar syrups can range in sweetness from extra light to extra heavy according to personal preference. If you wish to keep fruit inside the jar from floating to the top, use either light or medium sugar syrup.

Sugar Syrups

Type	Sugar	Water
Extra Light	1 cup	1 quart
Light	2 cups	1 quart
Medium	3 cups	1 quart
Heavy	4 cups	1 quart
Extra Heavy	5 cups	1 quart

To make simple syrup, combine sugar and water in a medium saucepan over medium heat until sugar crystals are dissolved. Raise the temperature to high and boil for 5 minutes. Keep warm until needed.

Hot Pack and Raw Pack Methods

The terms "hot pack" and "raw pack" refer to the manner which the contents are placed in the jar, either raw with liquid poured over it (raw pack) or cooked with liquid be packing in the jar (hot pack).

Delicate fruit, such as berries, will lose their shape if first cooked prior to canning. In their case, it is best to us the raw pack method, pouring hot liquid over the berries after they are gently placed into jars. Other fruits should simmered lightly for several minutes in the liquid of you choice prior to processing. This helps force some of the a trapped inside the fruit's tissues out, replacing it instead with liquid, thereby weighing the fruit down and removi the tendency for it to float to the top of the jar. If you wo prefer to use a heavy sugar syrup, water, or fruit juice, be advised that the fruit is more likely to float to the top of jar unless the hot pack method is used.

The amount of liquid each jar will require depends or the size of the fruit pieces, but generally runs between 3/ cup and 1 1/4 cups per pint. Canned fruit requires 1/2-inch (1.3 cm) headspace.

TIP:

It is absolutely essential that you always avoid using waxed produce in home canning. The wax coating makes it difficult for fluids to sufficientl penetrate the tissues of fruit and vegetables, posing the risk that deadly botulism spores may remain in produce even after pressure canning.

VEGETABLES

Imagine pints of corn, peas, and green beans lining pantry shelves, always at the ready for cooking up impromptu ca roles, stews, and soups. With a modest amount of effort, t vegetable fantasy can be your kitchen reality. Once canne and properly stored, vegetables no longer require refrigera tion or freezing, providing nonperishables for up to a year.

Preparation

Ideally, vegetables intended for canning should be preserved as close to harvest as possible. If you are canning vegetables you grew yourself, then you are, of course, in the best possible position to guarantee a speedy transit from harvest to jar. Otherwise, if you are purchasing produce from a farmers' market or roadside stand, inquire as to how long ago the vegetables were harvested. Deterioration begins just after harvesting, so acquiring the freshest produce possible is imperative.

If you develop a close relationship with the produce manager at your local grocer, it may be possible to learn when the vegetables available for purchase there were harvested. Wherever you source your produce from, give it a gentle scrub with a vegetable brush in a sink of cool water to remove any hidden dirt or debris. Change the soaking water several times if necessary. Any vegetables that float to the top (especially cucumbers) may be hollow and would be better used in recipes where they are chopped instead of being canned whole.

Canning Liquid

The liquid most often used for canning vegetables is simply water and salt. Adding salt helps the vegetables keep their consistency and flavor over time. If dietary sodium is a concern for you or your family, feel free to leave it out. Be advised, however, that vegetables canned without salt may lose a bit of color and become softer than those preserved with salt.

As with fruit, hot pack and raw pack methods may be used, although the hot pack method tends to produce better results with vegetables. Boil the vegetables in a bit of salted water for several minutes and then pack them into heated jars. Place the vegetables into the jars first and then ladle the hot liquid over them. Remember to leave headspace, which, in the case of vegetables, should be 1 inch (2.5 cm). Avoid overcrowding, as this can make it difficult for the water inside the jars to reach the temperature required to kill off nasty botulism spores.

When canning vegetables without added acid, you must process in a pressure canner. This is the only way to assure that botulism spores have been destroyed. Play it safe with vegetables and either pick up a pressure canner or acidify your veggies into relishes, pickles, chutneys, and salsas.

Choose the freshest produce available.

Troubleshooting Tips

Mistakes can be fabulous teachers. Sometimes you just don't know that you're doing something wrong until obvious clues present themselves. Once the error has been made, you know what not to do in the future, which only helps in making you a better home canner over time. The following is a guide for some of the most commonly occurring problems when canning whole fruit and vegetables.

If your jars fail to seal:

◘ You may have had some traces of the jar's contents on the rim. Always wipe the jar rim clean with a wet cloth before placing the lid and screw band on.

◘ You may not have had adequate water covering the tops of the jars in the boiling water bath. Be sure to have between 1 and 3 inches (2.5 and 7.6 cm) of water covering your jars at all times.

◘ You may have been using a jar with a cracked or chipped rim. Each time you can, check the rim of every jar by running your index finger around it before use.

◘ You may have left too much headspace in your jars. Leaving too much headspace can prevent a proper vacuum from forming, so always leave only the amount indicated in the recipe.

◘ You may have forgotten to adjust the processing time for altitude. If you live at an elevation above 1000 feet (300 m), remember to add on to processing times as necessary (refer to page 126 for altitude adjustment amounts).

If your jars leak during processing:

◘ You may have filled your jars too full. Remember to always leave enough headspace to account for expansion that occurs during processing.

◘ You may have crammed in too many fruits or vegetables. You want to pack the jar closely, but not too closely; there needs to be space for the preserving liquid to move in between the jar's contents.

If your jar's contents float to the top:

◘ You may have used the raw pack method for items needing be hot packed. For the most part, when canning fruit (except b ries) and vegetables, use the hot pack method.

◘ You may have used produce that wasn't properly ripened. When selecting fruit and vegetables for canning, look for ripened, yet firm, pieces.

If your jar's contents become cloudy:

◘ You may have used overripe produce. When selecting fruit a vegetables for canning, look for ripened, yet firm, pieces.

◘ You may have cooked your fruit or vegetables for too long in the preserving liquid before canning. Only cook your items for long as specified in the recipe before packing to jars. Use a tim if you think you might get distracted.

◘ You may have used table salt in your preserving liquid. Table sa contains fillers and anticaking agents that can cause liquids to be come cloudy. Use only pickling or kosher salt in the preserving liqu

◘ You may have failed to process your jars long enough to preve the growth of bacteria. Follow recipes stringently and according the processing manner they require. If the cloudiness is accomp nied by an off odor, dispose of the jar's contents without tasting.

If your food darkens at the top of the jar:

◘ You may have failed to put in an adequate amount of preser ing liquid. After placing the fruit or vegetables in the jar, ladle the preserving liquid over the contents until the proper amour of headspace is reached: ½ inch (1.3 cm) for fruit or 1 inch (2.5 cm) for vegetables.

◘ You may have failed to remove any trapped air bubbles in th jars. Always remember to use a nonmetallic tool for removing air bubbles around the interior circumference of the jars, befor wiping down the rims and applying the lids and screw bands.

◘ You may have left too much headspace in your jars. Leaving too much headspace can prevent a proper vacuum from formin so always leave only the amount indicated in the recipe.

◘ You may have failed to process your jars long enough to kill off enzymes. Follow processing times exactly as written in the recipe, adjusting as necessary for altitude.

Portrait of a Canner

Amy

Although she's been canning for as long as she can remember, it was a recent trip to France that got Amy truly ready to pump up the jams. Finding herself enamored of the small-production, artisan jams sprinkled throughout markets in that country's quaint south, she returned home determined to master the process of putting up jam herself. When a co-worker showed up with 50 pounds of peaches, "a jam business was born."

Now producing her own line of small-batch jams made in the French tradition, Amy sells her Lemon Bird Handmade Jams online. Operating just outside the metropolitan area of Los Angeles, she utilizes area farmers' markets to source her jams' ingredients. From blood oranges, kumquats, lemons, strawberries, and cherries to peaches, apricots, figs, berries, pears, and even tomatoes, Amy shops seasonally, buying the best from family farmers she has come to know personally. She's even dubbed a few of them her "favorite farmers," as they grow some of the most delicious produce she's ever eaten.

Having grown up eating—and canning—the produce grown in her family's large backyard garden, as well as that available on nearby farms, Amy is no stranger to the alchemy of home canning. With a jam business of her own, she's been able to both cultivate her love of the preservation technique as well as patronize the family farms she holds so dear. It is her fondest wish that the jams she concocts serve to benefit producers and consumers alike. "Hopefully, home canning and preserving will help to carry on the eating of seasonal and natural foods, while supporting those that grow and produce our foods."

Whole, Crushed, or Quartered Tomatoes

If you're looking for an ideal way to pack away the exquisite taste of one of summer's most beloved fruits, look no further. In a few short steps you'll be on your way to enjoying tomato deliciousness year-round.

This recipe is graciously provided by Chris, who you can read more about in his profile on page 78.

Yield: 12 to 14 pints

YOU WILL NEED:

18 to 20 pounds meaty tomatoes, such as Roma

Bottled lemon juice or citric acid powder

Pickling salt

Pressure Canner

TO PREPARE:

1. Wash 14 pint-sized mason jars, lids, and screw rings (refer to page 29 for detailed instructions). Remember to inspect the jars for cracks, chips, or scratches, and ensure that the screw bands are rust-free. Although you don't need to sterilize jars that will be pressure canned, you will need your jars to be hot when filled in order to prevent them from cracking. You can either run the jars through the dishwasher, keeping them warm until ready for use, or place jars in a stockpot or boiling water bath canner, cover with water, and keep simmering until ready for use.

2. Wash tomatoes. Make a small crosshatch score across the bottom of each fruit. Fill a large metal bowl with ice water, and place in the sink.

3. Put the rack in the bottom of the pressure canner, fill with 2 to 3 inches (5 to 7.6 cm) of water, and set over low heat (adjust as needed, according to the manufacturer's instructions for your model). With the lid off, bring just to the boiling point. Place the jar lids in a small saucepan, fill with water, bring to a boil, turn off the heat, and leave on the stovetop until needed.

4. Bring a large pot of water to a boil over high heat. Drop the tomatoes into boiling water for 30 to 60 seconds, or until the skins split. Using a slotted spoon, ladle the tomatoes into the ice water bath. When they are cool enough to handle, slip off the skins and cut out the cores. Depending on your preference, quarter, halve, or leave tomatoes whole.

5. Place the hot mason jars on top of a kitchen cloth on the counter. Into each jar, place ½ teaspoon salt and either 1 tablespoon bottled lemon juice or ¼ teaspoon citric acid powder.

6. With the help of a canning funnel, pack tomatoes tightly and evenly into the jars, reserving ½-inch (1.3 cm) headspace. Use a nonmetallic spatula to remove any trapped air bubbles, ensuring that all voids in the jar are filled with juice. Wipe the rims clean with a damp cloth. Place on the lids and screw bands, tightening only until fingertip-tight.

7. Using a jar lifter, place the jars in the canner. Remember to exhaust the vent first. Process at 15 pounds (6.8 kg) pressure for 15 minutes if using a weighted-gauge canner, or at 11 pounds (5 kg) pressure for 25 minutes if using a dial-gauge canner (refer to page 34 for detailed instructions). Remember to adjust for altitude.

A jar funnel can be a great time saver.

Whole Peaches

Nothing says summertime quite like peaches. With home canning, you can enjoy the taste of peaches when autumn leaves cover the ground, snow blankets the streets, and buds burst into bloom. Make sure your peaches are at the peak of ripeness and bruise-free in order to capture these heady fruits at their finest. *Yield: 6 pints or 3 quarts*

YOU WILL NEED:

- 8 pounds peaches
- 3 cups granulated sugar
- Antibrowning solution (see page 83)

TO PREPARE:

1. Sterilize 6 pint- or 3 quart-sized mason jars, lids, and screw rings (refer to page 29 for detailed instructions).

2. Fill a canner or large stockpot with water and set over medium-high heat. Bring just to the boiling point. Place the jar lids in a small saucepan, fill with water, bring to a boil, turn off the heat, and set the pan aside.

3. Combine the sugar and 4 cups water in medium saucepan over medium heat until all sugar crystals are dissolved. Raise the heat to high, and boil for 5 minutes. Keep the syrup warm until needed for packing.

4. Blanch the peaches (refer to "Prep School" on page 52 for detailed blanching instructions). When they are cool enough to handle, cut the peaches in half and remove the pits. Add the peaches to an antibrowning solution as you prep them. Once all the peaches are prepped, drain and rinse the fruit completely to remove any traces of antibrowning solution.

5. Add the peaches to the sugar syrup, and warm over medium-high heat for 2 minutes. Remove the peaches with a slotted spoon, and pack into hot jars; ladle sugar syrup over the peaches until covered, reserving ½-inch (1.3 cm) headspace.

6. Process pint jars for 20 minutes and quart jars for 25 minutes in a boiling water bath (refer to page 32 for detailed instructions). Remember to adjust for altitude.

Variations: Instead of sugar syrup, you can use 100% white grape or apple juice as the preserving liquid. To imbue your peaches with a subtle spiciness, add one cinnamon stick, two whole cloves, and two whole allspice to each jar. These peaches, evocative of a Middle Eastern spice bazaar, would be heavenly paired with fresh whipped cream, rice pudding, vanilla ice cream, or alongside a warm slice of coffee cake.

Smothered in butter, nestled into cornbread, or tucked into succotash, everything really does seem to go better with crunchy, sweet kernels of corn. When the season is high and corn can be found fresh at farmer's markets, local grocers, and backyards, grab a bushel or two and put up several pints. The reward is being able to brew up a steaming pot of corn chowder anytime! As the sugars in corn quickly turn to starch, plan on processing your ears as close to harvest time as possible, otherwise the corn begins losing some of its sweetness. *Yield: 6 pints or 3 quarts*

YOU WILL NEED:

- 16 ears sweet corn
- 4 cups boiling water
- Pressure Canner

TO PREPARE:

1. Husk the corn, remove the silk, and wash the ears under cool water. Using a sharp knife (a serrated knife works quite well), cut the kernels off the cob, taking care not to cut into the cob itself. Place into a bowl, and set aside.

2. Wash 6 pint or 3 quart-sized mason jars, lids, and screw rings (refer to page 29 for detailed instructions). Remember to inspect jars for cracks, chips, or scratches, and ensure that screw bands are rust-free. Although you don't need to sterilize jars that will be pressure canned, you will need your jars to be hot when filled in order to prevent them from cracking. You can either run the jars through the dishwasher, keeping them warm until ready for use, or place the jars in a stockpot or boiling water bath canner, cover with water, and keep simmering until ready for use.

3. Put a rack in the bottom of your pressure canner, fill with 2 to 3 inches (5 to 7.6 cm) of water, and set over low heat (adjust as needed, according to the manufacturers'

instructions for your model). With the lid off, bring water just to the boiling point. Place lids in a small saucepan, fill with water, bring to a boil, turn off the heat, and leave on the stovetop until needed.

4. Combine the corn and 4 cups water in a large saucepan. Bring to a boil, reduce heat to medium-high, and simmer for 4 minutes. Remove the saucepan from the heat and drain corn, reserving liquid.

5. Place the hot jars on top of a kitchen cloth on the counter. With the help of a canning funnel and slotted spoon, pack corn evenly into the jars, leaving 1-inch (2.5 cm) headspace. Take care not to press the corn down or pack too tightly.

6. Ladle reserved cooking liquid over the corn, again leaving 1-inch (2.5 cm) headspace. Use a nonmetallic spatula to remove any trapped air bubbles, and wipe the rims clean with a damp cloth. Adjust headspace, if necessary, by adding more hot water. Place on the lids and screw bands, tightening only until fingertip-tight.

7. Using a jar lifter, place jars in the pressure canner. Remember to exhaust the vent. Process pints for 55 minutes and quarts for 85 minutes, selecting 11 pounds (5 kg) of pressure for dial-gauge models or 10 pounds (4.5 kg) of pressure for weighted-gauge models (refer to page 34 for detailed instructions). Remember to adjust for altitude.

Chapter 8
Seasonal Recipes

Where matters of taste are concerned, freshness counts. Flavor and nutrients are at their best when fruits and vegetables are allowed to ripen on the vine. When at all possible, it's best to purchase your produce locally and in season. That said, if you can't find truly local produce, consider purchasing fruit and vegetables brought in from a few states away rather than those from across the country or the globe. Above all else, remember to always choose the best specimens you encounter. Your end products can only be as good as the ingredients you begin with.

❄ Winter

Glowing fireplaces, mugs of hot chocolate, and quiet evenings spent indoors, preferably under the protection of a cozy blanket, are hallmarks of winter. While the season presents limited offerings fresh from the garden, it does herald the arrival of a number of citrus fruits that thrive in a light chill. Kumquats, blood oranges, clementines, and grapefruit are at their ripest and most mouthwatering, offering a bright counterpoint to the drabness of the season. Winter squashes, harvested and stored in autumn, are also available in abundance, as are cold-hardy crops such as fennel, Brussels sprouts, and kale. The chill outdoors is also fabulous motivation for warming up the kitchen, so wash up the mason jars and bring some much-needed heat to hearts and bellies.

Clementine Cointreau Curd

$\mathbf{F}$ew seasonal treats are as dazzling, or as ephemeral, as clementines. Packed in don't-blink-or-you'll-miss-them wooden crates, these sweet yet puckery citrus fruits make a brief cameo during cooler months. Try this curd atop currant scones, tucked into pastry shells, or sandwiched between layers of poppy seed cake. *Yield: 3 half-pints*

YOU WILL NEED:	
5	clementines
4	eggs
1¼	cups superfine sugar
10	tablespoons unsalted butter, chilled
2	tablespoons Cointreau
	Pressure Canner

TO PREPARE:

1. Wash 3 half-pint mason jars, lids, and screw rings (refer to page 29 for detailed instructions). Remember to inspect the jars for cracks, chips, or scratches, and ensure that screw bands are rust-free. Although you don't need to sterilize jars that will be pressure canned, you will need your jars to be hot when filled in order to prevent them from cracking. You can either run the jars through the dishwasher, keeping them warm until ready for use, or place the jars in a stockpot or boiling water bath canner, cover with water, and keep simmering until ready for use.

2. Put a jar rack in the bottom of the pressure canner. Fill the canner with 2 to 3 inches (5 to 7.6 cm) of water and set over low heat (adjust as needed according to the manufacturer's instructions for your model). With the lid off, bring just to the boiling point. Place the jar lids in a small saucepan, fill with water, bring to a boil, turn off the heat, and leave on the stovetop until needed.

3. Wash and dry the clementines, then zest them, taking care to avoid removing any pith along with the zest. Juice the fruits, and strain the juice through a fine-mesh sieve to remove any membrane or seeds. Set the zest and juice aside.

4. Place the eggs in a medium metal bowl, and beat lightly to incorporate the whites into the yolks.

5. Fill a medium saucepan with about 2 inches (5 cm) of water, and place it over medium heat. Bring to a gentle simmer. Place the egg bowl on top of the pan to form a double boiler, and add the sugar, butter, Cointreau, clementine juice, and zest. Whisk gently until the sugar dissolves and the butter melts.

6. Stir the mixture with a wooden spoon until it thickens and coats the back of the spoon, 8 to 10 minutes. Remove the curd from the heat.

7. Place the jars on top of a kitchen cloth on the counter. With the help of a canning funnel, ladle curd into the jars, reserving ¼-inch (6 mm) headspace. Use a non-metallic spatula to remove any trapped air bubbles, and wipe the rims clean with a damp cloth. Place on the lids and screw bands, tightening only until fingertip-tight.

8. Using a jar lifter, place the jars in the pressure canner. Remember to exhaust the vent. Process for 10 minutes at 11 pounds (5 kg) pressure for a dial-gauge canner or at 10 pounds (4.5 kg) pressure for a weighted-gauge canner (refer to page 34 for detailed instructions). Remember to adjust for altitude.

Variation: To make this curd without alcohol, replace the Cointreau with orange juice. You can also substitute mandarin oranges for the clementines.

Kumquat 5-Spice Marmalad

This tiny citrus fruit is one of the only varieties that can be eaten whole, peel and all. Oftentimes, its peel is actually sweeter than its fruit. Punctuated with exotic spices, this marmalade will warm up even the coldest of winter breakfast tables. **Yield: 5 pints**

5 pints kumquats

Cheesecloth or a muslin tea bag

6 cups granulated sugar

1 2/3 cups water

3 1/2 teaspoons bottled lemon juice

1 tablespoon Chinese 5-spice powder (see tip)

TIP:

If you can't find Chinese 5-spice powder at your local grocer, you can easily make your own at home. Toast 1 tablespoon black peppercorns over low heat until fragrant. Remove from heat, and place in a coffee grinder or spice mill. Add 3 whole star anise and 1 tablespoon fennel seed. Grind the spices until they are powdered. Sift the mixture through a fine-mesh sieve over a mixing bowl to remove any large pieces of spices. Add 1 tablespoon ground cinnamon and 1 teaspoon ground cloves, and stir gently to combine.

TO PREPARE:

1. Place two small plates in the freezer (these will be used later to test for gelling).

2. Thinly slice the kumquats, removing and reserving any seeds. The seeds contain a good deal of pectin and will help to thicken the marmalade. Place the seeds in a 4-inch (10.2 cm) square of cheesecloth or a muslin tea bag.

If using cheesecloth, twist up all 4 corners and secure with a rubber band or kitchen twine; if using a muslin tea bag, cinch ties securely.

3. Put the seed bag, kumquat slices, sugar, water, lemon juice, and 5-spice powder in a large, heavy, stainless-steel saucepan. Bring to a boil over medium-high heat. Reduce the heat to low and simmer for 25 minutes, stirring frequently to keep from sticking.

4. Meanwhile, sterilize 5 pint-sized mason jars, lids, and screw rings (refer to page 29 for detailed instructions). Fill a canner or large stockpot with water, and set over medium-high heat. Bring just to the boiling point. Place the jar lids in a small saucepan, fill with water, bring to a boil, turn off the heat, and set the pan aside.

5. Next, test the marmalade for gelling. Remove a plate from the freezer, and spoon about 1 teaspoon of hot marmalade onto it. Place the plate back in the freezer, and wait 2 minutes. Remove it from the freezer, and push the edge of the marmalade with your fingertip. If it has gelled properly, the surface will wrinkle a bit. If it fails to wrinkle, or is obviously still runny, continue cooking the marmalade for 5 minutes longer, and then repeat the test.

6. Place the hot jars on top of a kitchen cloth on the counter. Remove the seed bag from the marmalade, squeezing with a spoon to remove any juices. With the help of a canning funnel, pack marmalade into the jars, reserving 1/4-inch (6 mm) headspace. Use a nonmetallic spatula to remove any trapped air bubbles, and wipe the rims clean with a damp cloth. Place on the lids and screw bands, tightening only until fingertip-tight.

7. Using a jar lifter, place the jars in the canner. Process 15 minutes in a boiling water bath (refer to page 32 for detailed instructions). Remember to adjust for altitude.

Variation: For a more traditional kumquat marmalade, omit the 5-spice powder. If you prefer just a hint of spice, add 1 teaspoon ground cinnamon.

Curried Winter Squash Chutney

Here's a fabulous way to preserve all those gorgeous winter squashes! Serve this chutney as a spread on hearty sandwiches, alongside roast chicken or pot roast, or simply slathered onto a crusty hunk of bread.
Yield: 5 pints

YOU WILL NEED:

Cheesecloth or a muslin tea bag

5 cardamom pods

1 teaspoon whole cumin seed

1 teaspoon whole cloves

1 teaspoon whole yellow mustard seed

2 teaspoons black peppercorns

1 teaspoon fenugreek seed*

2 teaspoons whole coriander seed

1 cinnamon stick

4 pounds acorn, butternut, or kabocha squash, peeled, seeded, and diced

3 medium cooking apples, peeled, cored, and diced

2 large yellow onions, peeled and diced

1 cup raisins

1 cup currants

1½ cups granulated sugar

½ cup dark brown sugar

2½ cups cider vinegar

1½ cups water

½ teaspoon salt

1 teaspoon ground fenugreek*

1 teaspoon ground ginger

2 teaspoons brown mustard seed

1 teaspoon ground cinnamon

*Fenugreek is available at most large grocery stores, as well as many natural foods stores.

TO PREPARE:

1. You'll begin by creating a spice bag. If using cheesecloth, cut out a 4-inch (10.2 cm) square. Put the cardamom pods, cumin seed, whole cloves, yellow mustard seed, black peppercorns, fenugreek seed, coriander seed, and cinnamon stick in the center of the cheesecloth, twist up all 4 corners, and secure with a rubber band or kitchen twine. If using a muslin tea bag, simply place these spices inside and cinch the top.

2. Place the spice bag, squash, apples, onion, raisins, currants, sugars, vinegar, water, salt, ground fenugreek, ground ginger, brown mustard seed, and ground cinnamon in a large, heavy, stainless-steel saucepan. Bring the mixture to a gentle boil over medium heat, and cook uncovered for 45 minutes. Stir frequently to prevent the mixture from sticking. If additional liquid is necessary, add water in ¼ cup increments.

3. While the chutney cooks, sterilize 5 pint-sized mason jars, lids, and screw rings (refer to page 29 for detailed instructions). Fill a canner or large stockpot with water, and set it over medium-high heat. Bring just to the boiling point. Place the lids in a small saucepan, fill with water, bring to a boil, turn off the heat, and set the pan aside.

4. Place the hot jars on top of a kitchen cloth on the counter. Remove the spice bag from the chutney. With the help of a canning funnel, pack chutney into the jars, reserving ½-inch (1.3 cm) headspace. Use a nonmetallic spatula to remove any trapped air bubbles, and wipe the rims clean with a damp cloth. Place on the lids and screw bands, tightening only until fingertip-tight.

5. Using a jar lifter, place the jars in the canner. Process 15 minutes in a boiling water bath (refer to page 32 for detailed instructions). Remember to adjust for altitude.
Variation: Replace the winter squash with an equal amount of sugar pie pumpkin.

Fennel Relish

This licorice-y bulb introduces unexpected pizzazz to an otherwise traditional relish. This relish would make a fabulous addition to a winter cheese plate, paired with strong cheeses and peppery crackers. It would also marry well with cold cuts for a lively sandwich. *Yield: 4 pints*

YOU WILL NEED:

2 fennel bulbs

2 red bell peppers, seeded and thinly sliced

1 large sweet onion (Vidalia or Walla Walla), thinly sliced

Pickling or kosher salt

2/3 cup granulated sugar

3 cups white vinegar

1 1/2 cups water

Black peppercorns

Bay leaves

Caraway seed

TO PREPARE:

1. Wash the fennel bulbs and gently scrub them with a vegetable brush. Pat them dry. Slice each bulb in half lengthwise, remove the fronds and core, and slice thin into half-moons. Combine the fennel slices with the re pepper and onion slices in a large glass or ceramic bow Sprinkle with 4 1/2 teaspoons salt, toss to mix, cover loo ly with a kitchen cloth, and let rest at room temperatu for up to four hours or overnight in the refrigerator.

2. Sterilize 4 pint-sized mason jars, lids, and screw rings (refer to page 29 for detailed instructions). Fill a canner or large stockpot with water, and set over medium-high heat. Bring just to the boiling point. Pla the jar lids in a small saucepan, fill with water, bring boil, turn off the heat, and set the pan aside.

3. Drain and rinse the fennel mixture thoroughly in colander. Set aside. Combine the sugar, vinegar, water and 1 1/2 teaspoons salt in a heavy, medium stainless-steel saucepan. Bring the brine to a boil over medium high heat. Add the fennel mixture, return to a gentle b and cook for 2 minutes. Remove from heat.

4. Place the hot jars on top of a kitchen cloth on the counter. Into each jar, place 1 teaspoon black pepper-corns, 1 bay leaf, and 1/2 teaspoon caraway seed. With the help of a canning funnel and a slotted spoon, pack the fennel mixture evenly into the jars. Ladle brine ove the vegetables, leaving 1/2-inch (1.3 cm) headspace. Use nonmetallic spatula to remove any trapped air bubbles and wipe the rims clean with a damp cloth. Place on th lids and screw bands, tightening only until fingertip-ti

5. Using a jar lifter, place the jars in the canner. Process minutes in a boiling water bath (refer to page 32 for deta instructions). Remember to adjust for altitude if needed. **Variation:** Replace fennel with 2 1/2 cups shredded red cabbage.

Blood Orange and Port Sauce

Sweet-tart blood oranges meld seamlessly with the nuttiness of tawny port. This sauce is infinitely versatile, jazzing up any meal you serve it with. Try it over cornmeal pancakes, as a poaching liquid for dried fruits, or simply drizzled over almond or sponge cake.

Yield: 6 half-pints

YOU WILL NEED:

- 6 cups blood orange segments (from about 9 oranges), pith and seeds removed
- 1/2 cup tawny port
- 3/4 cup orange juice
- 3/4 cup granulated sugar
- 1 teaspoon ground cinnamon
- 1/2 teaspoon ground nutmeg
- 1/2 teaspoon ground cloves

TO PREPARE:

1. Sterilize 6 half-pint mason jars, lids, and screw rings (refer to page 29 for detailed instructions). Fill a canner or large stockpot with water, and set over medium-high heat. Bring just to the boiling point. Place the lids in a small saucepan, fill with water, bring to a boil, turn off the heat, and set the pan aside.

2. Pulse the blood orange segments briefly in a food processor or blender until just barely puréed. Set aside.

3. To a large, heavy, stainless-steel saucepan, add the port, orange juice, sugar, and spices. Bring the mixture to a boil over medium-high heat, and cook until the sugar is completely dissolved. Add the blood orange puree, reduce the heat to low, and simmer for 10 minutes, stirring occasionally with a wooden spoon. Remove from heat.

4. Place the hot jars on top of a kitchen cloth on the counter. With the help of a canning funnel, ladle the sauce into the jars, reserving 1/4-inch (6 mm) headspace. Use a nonmetallic spatula to remove any trapped air bubbles, and wipe the rims clean with a damp cloth. Place on the lids and screw bands, tightening only until fingertip-tight.

5. Using a jar lifter, place the jars in the canner. Process 10 minutes in a boiling water bath (refer to page 32 for detailed instructions). Remember to adjust for altitude.

Variation: For an alcohol-free version, replace the port with an equal amount of pomegranate juice. You can also substitute tangerines for the blood oranges.

Spring

The thaw is coming. You can feel it in your bones and smell it in your nose. The birds are chirping a bit more loudly, tiny frogs are tentatively trying out their emerging voices, daffodils bravely punctuate the landscape with bursts of yellow, and tender buds emerge from sleepy branches. Spring is all about renewal, vitality, and perseverance. At the market and in backyard gardens, faithful perennials like rhubarb and asparagus shake off winter's vestiges and rise from the soil. Strawberries and apricots offer rhapsody in every bite. Breathe in the freshness, soak up the sun, and spring back into action!

Strawberry and Vanilla Sauce

Few fruits shout "spring has come" like strawberries. Coupled with vanilla bean, as it is here, the fruit easily transforms from humble to majestic. Try this sauce drizzled over vanilla ice cream, Belgian waffles, or angel food cake. **Yield: 6 half-pints**

- 5 pints strawberries, hulled and sliced
- 1³⁄4 cups granulated sugar
- 1 cup water
- 3 tablespoons bottled lemon juice
- 1 vanilla bean, sliced lengthwise

TO PREPARE:

1. Sterilize 6 half-pint mason jars, lids, and screw rings (refer to page 29 for detailed instructions). Fill a canner or large stockpot with water, and set over medium-high heat. Bring just to the boiling point. Place the lids in a small saucepan, fill with water, bring to a boil, turn off the heat, and set the pan aside.

2. Measure out 3 cups of sliced strawberries into a medium glass or ceramic bowl. With a potato masher, crush gently.

3. Combine the sugar and water in a heavy, medium stainless-steel saucepan over low heat. Stir continually until the sugar is completely dissolved. Add the crushed strawberries, bring to a boil, then reduce heat and simmer for 7 minutes. Stir frequently to prevent sticking.

4. Add the remaining strawberries to the pan, along with the lemon juice. Using a paring knife or fork tine, scrape the seeds from the vanilla bean into the pan. Remove pod; you can use the pod to make vanilla sugar or steep in vodka.

5. Bring the mixture back to a gentle boil and cook for 3 minutes, stirring constantly. Remove from the heat.

6. Place the hot jars on top of a kitchen cloth on the counter. Ladle sauce into the jars, reserving ½-inch (1.3 cm) headspace. Use a nonmetallic spatula to remove any trapped air bubbles, and wipe the rims clean with a damp cloth. Place on the lids and screw bands, tightening only until fingertip-tight.

7. Using a jar lifter, place the jars in the canner. Process 10 minutes in a boiling water bath (refer to page 32 for detailed instructions). Remember to adjust for altitude.

Variation: For an unexpected herbal note, replace the vanilla bean with 2 sprigs of fresh rosemary. Remove and discard before bottling.

Meyer Lemon and Lemon Verbena Curd

Meyer lemons are a cross between traditional lemons and mandarin oranges. Sweeter and less acidic than their conventional cousins, with a softer peel, Meyer lemons are perfectly suited to curds. Lemon verbena punches up the citrus a few more notes, presenting a flavor and fragrance that are quintessentially spring. *Yield: 3 half-pints*

- 6 Meyer lemons
- 4 eggs
- 2 cups superfine sugar
- 10 tablespoons unsalted butter, chilled
- 2 teaspoons fresh lemon verbena, chopped (1 teaspoon dried)

Pressure Canner

TO PREPARE:

1. Wash 3 half-pint mason jars, lids, and screw rings (refer to page 29 for detailed instructions). Remember to inspect the jars for cracks, chips, or scratches, and ensure that screw bands are rust-free. Although you don't need to sterilize jars that will be pressure canned, you will need your jars to be hot when filled in order to prevent them from cracking. You can either run the jars through the dishwasher, keeping them warm until ready for use, or place the jars in a stockpot or boiling water bath canner, cover with water, and keep simmering until ready for use.

2. Put a jar rack in the bottom of your pressure canner, fill the pot with 2 to 3 inches (5 to 7.6 cm) of water, and set it over low heat (adjust as needed according to the manufacturer's instructions for your model). With the lid off, bring just to the boiling point. Place the lids in a small saucepan, fill with water, bring to a boil, turn off the heat, and leave on the stovetop until needed.

3. Wash and dry the Meyer lemons, then zest them, taking care to avoid removing any pith along with the zest. Next, juice the fruits and strain the juice over a fine-mesh sieve to remove any membranes or seeds. Set the zest and juice aside.

4. Crack the eggs into a medium metal bowl, and beat lightly to incorporate the whites into the yolks.

5. Fill a medium saucepan with about 2 inches (5 cm) of water, and bring to a gentle simmer over medium heat. Put the metal bowl on top of the pan to form a double boiler, and add the sugar, butter, lemon verbena, Meyer lemon juice, and zest. Whisk gently until the sugar dissolves and the butter melts.

6. Stir the mixture until it thickens and coats the back of a wooden spoon, about 8 to 10 minutes. Remove the curd from the heat.

7. Place the jars on top of a kitchen cloth on the counter. With the help of a canning funnel, ladle curd into the jars, reserving 1/4-inch (6 mm) headspace. Use a nonmetallic spatula to remove any trapped air bubbles, and wipe the rims clean with a damp cloth. Place on the lids and screw bands, tightening only until fingertip-tight.

8. Using a jar lifter, place the jars in the pressure canner. Remember to exhaust the vent. Process for 10 minutes at 11 pounds (5 kg) pressure for a dial-gauge canner or 10 pounds (4.5 kg) pressure for a weighted-gauge canner (refer to page 34 for detailed instructions). Remember to adjust for altitude.
Variation: For a more traditional curd, omit the lemon verbena. Alternatively, replace the lemon verbena with an equal amount of fresh mint. You can also substitute regular lemons for the Meyer lemons.

Rhubarb and Amaretto Chutney

Technically a vegetable, rhubarb is often used as a fruit. Only the stalks are eaten, as the leaves are poisonous. Its flavor is characteristically tart, which is why it is usually prepared with added sugar. Here the scarlet-tinged perennial is paired with amaretto, citrus, and spices to create a tart and piquant spread. Try it over seared fish or as a topping for bruschetta. *Yield: 5 half-pints*

YOU WILL NEED:

	Cheesecloth or a muslin tea bag
5	cardamom pods
1	teaspoon whole cumin seed
1	teaspoon whole cloves
1	teaspoon whole yellow mustard seed
2	teaspoons black peppercorns
2	teaspoons whole coriander seed
1	whole cinnamon stick
5	cups rhubarb, chopped
3¾	cups light brown sugar
2½	cups sweet onions (Vidalia or Walla Walla), chopped
1	cup seedless raisins
3	cloves garlic, minced
1	tablespoon gingerroot, minced
2½	cups apple cider vinegar
½	cup amaretto
2	tablespoons lemon zest
2	teaspoons ground cinnamon
½	teaspoon ground cloves
1	tablespoon yellow mustard seed
1½	teaspoons pickling or kosher salt

TO PREPARE:

1. Begin by creating a spice bag. If using cheesecloth, cut out a 4-inch (10.2 cm) square. Put the cardamom pods, cumin seed, whole cloves, yellow mustard seed, black peppercorns, coriander seed, and cinnamon stick in the center of the cheesecloth, twist up all 4 corners, and secure with a rubber band or kitchen twine. If using a muslin tea bag, simply place these spices inside and cinch the top.

2. Place the spice bag, rhubarb, brown sugar, onions, raisins, garlic, ginger, and vinegar in a large, heavy, stainless-steel saucepan. Bring to a gentle boil over medium heat and cook, uncovered, for 30 minutes. Add the amaretto, lemon zest, ground cinnamon, ground cloves, yellow mustard seed, and salt. Simmer an additional 30 minutes, stirring frequently to prevent sticking. If additional liquid is necessary, add water in ¼ cup increments if chutney begins to stick to the pot.

3. While the chutney cooks, sterilize 5 half-pint mason jars, lids, and screw rings (refer to page 29 for detailed instructions). Fill a canner or large stockpot with water, and set over medium-high heat. Bring just to the boiling point. Place the lids in a small saucepan, fill with water, bring to a boil, remove from the heat, and set the pan aside.

4. Place the hot jars on top of a kitchen cloth on the counter. With the help of a canning funnel, pack chutney into the jars, reserving ½-inch (1.3 cm) headspace. Use a nonmetallic spatula to remove any trapped air bubbles, and wipe the rims clean with a damp cloth. Place on the lids and screw bands, tightening only until fingertip-tight.

5. Using a jar lifter, place the jars in the canner. Process 10 minutes in a boiling water bath (refer to page 32 for detailed instructions). Remember to adjust for altitude.

Variation: For an alcohol-free version, replace the amaretto with an equal amount of orange juice, in which case you might also want to use orange zest instead of lemon zest.

Herbed Pickled Asparagus

The asparagus spear is the unofficial official harbinger of spring. Poking up from soil that previously held no signs of activity underfoot, asparagus springs forth like an ambassador of hope and greener pastures ahead. Pickling the tender spears is a fabulous way of enjoying the promise of rebirth and renewal. *Yield: 4 pints*

YOU WILL NEED:

- 3 pounds fresh asparagus
- 2½ cups white wine vinegar
- 2 cups water
- 2 tablespoons granulated sugar
- 1½ teaspoons pickling or kosher salt
- 4 sprigs fresh oregano
- 4 sprigs fresh marjoram

TO PREPARE:

1. Sterilize 4 pint-sized mason jars, lids, and screw rings (refer to page 29 for detailed instructions). Fill a canner or lar stockpot with water, and set over medium-high heat. Bring jus to the boiling point. Place the lids in a small saucepan, fill wit water, bring to a boil, turn off the heat, and set the pan aside.

2. Wash the asparagus and trim each spear to 4 inches (10.2 cm). Quickly blanch the asparagus by placing in boilir water for 1 minute, then immediately plunging into an ice-water bath. Remove from water and pat dry.

3. In a heavy, medium stainless-steel saucepan over mediun heat, combine the vinegar, water, sugar, and salt. Bring the brir solution just to the boiling point, cover, and remove from heat.

4. Place the hot jars on top of a kitchen cloth on the count Pack the asparagus spears into the jars. Add 1 sprig of orega and 1 sprig of marjoram to each jar. With the help of a canni funnel, ladle brining solution evenly over the asparagus, res ing ½-inch (1.3 cm) headspace. Use a nonmetallic spatula to remove any trapped air bubbles, and wipe the rims clean wi damp cloth. Place on the lids and screw bands, tightening on until fingertip-tight.

5. Using a jar lifter, place the jars in the canner. Process 20 minutes in a boiling water bath (refer to page 32 for detailed instructions). Remember to adjust for altitude. **Variation:** To make a more traditional pickle, replace the oregano and marjoram with 1½ teaspoons dill seed and 1 sprig fresh dill in each jar.

Apricot Jam

Apricots are enjoyed by cultures as far-flung and diverse as India, Japan, Iran, and the United States. Their international pedigree no doubt owes to the fruit's winning combination of heady aroma, sweet flesh, and edible skin. This jam is about as easy as they come, pairing perfectly with cuisines from every continent. *Yield: 4 half-pints*

YOU WILL NEED:

3 pounds fresh apricots

4 cups granulated sugar

1/3 cup bottled lemon juice

TO PREPARE:

1. Cut the apricots in half, remove the pits, and chop the fruit coarsely. Combine the fruit, sugar, and lemon juice in a ceramic or glass bowl, cover loosely with a kitchen cloth, and leave at room temperature for 2 hours.

2. Place 2 small plates in the freezer (these will be used later to test for gelling).

3. Sterilize 4 half-pint mason jars, lids, and screw rings (refer to page 29 for detailed instructions). Fill a canner or large stockpot with water, and set over medium-high heat. Bring just to the boiling point. Place the lids in a small saucepan, fill with water, bring to a boil, turn off the heat, and set the saucepan aside.

4. Place the apricot mixture in a large, heavy, stainless-steel saucepan, and bring to a boil over medium-high heat. Reduce the heat to medium and simmer gently for 20 to 25 minutes, until the jam begins to gel. Use a slotted spoon or skimmer to remove any foam that forms on the top of the jam as it cooks.

5. Test for gelling. Remove a plate from the freezer, and spoon about 1 teaspoon of the jam onto it. Place the plate back in the freezer, and wait 2 minutes. Remove it from the freezer, and push the edge of the jam with your fingertip. If it has gelled properly, the surface will wrinkle a bit. If it fails to wrinkle, or is obviously still runny, continue cooking the jam for 5 minutes longer, and then repeat the test.

6. Place the hot jars on top of a kitchen cloth on the counter. With the help of a canning funnel, pack jam into the jars, reserving 1/2-inch (1.3 cm) headspace. Use a nonmetallic spatula to remove any trapped air bubbles, and wipe the rims clean with a damp cloth. Place on the lids and screw bands, tightening only until fingertip-tight.

7. Using a jar lifter, place the jars in the canner. Process 10 minutes in a boiling water bath (refer to page 32 for detailed instructions). Remember to adjust for altitude.

Variation: For a hint of spice, add 1/2 teaspoon nutmeg, freshly grated, if possible; otherwise, bottled ground nutmeg works perfectly fine.

Summer

Summer is the busiest season for home canners, and for good reason. While lazy picnics, afternoon naps, and cool beverages sing their siren songs, the garden's bounty demands attention. Cherries, peaches, and nectarines are looking for hands to stain and mouths to please, while tomatoes and fresh herbs multiply with abandon. Fire up the water bath or pressure canner, slip into something made of cotton, pour yourself a cool glass of lemonade, and do your best to put up with summer!

Nectarine Chutney

Choose white or yellow nectarines for this seasonal condiment. Enjoy with a bagel and cream cheese, in a turkey sandwich, or with a warm piece of buttered naan.

Yield: 4 pints

YOU WILL NEED:

- 3 pounds nectarines
- 1 large sweet onion (Vidalia or Walla Walla), chopped
- 1/4 cup fresh cherries, chopped (1/3 cup dried)
- 1 cup raisins
- 1/2 cup golden raisins
- 4 garlic cloves, minced
- 1 tablespoon fresh ginger, grated
- 2 cups light brown sugar
- 3 1/2 cups apple cider vinegar
- 1 tablespoon mustard seed
- 1 1/2 teaspoons crushed red pepper flakes
- 1 teaspoon ground cinnamon

TO PREPARE:

1. Blanch the nectarines following the instructions on page 52. Once the fruit is cool enough to handle, peel, pit, and chop roughly.

2. Place all the ingredients in a large, heavy, stainless-steel saucepan. Bring the mixture to a boil over medium-high heat. Stir continually until the sugar is completely dissolved. Reduce the heat to low and simmer uncovered for 45 minutes, stirring frequently to keep from sticking. If additional liquid is necessary, add water in 1/4 cup increments.

3. While the chutney cooks, sterilize 4 pint-sized mason jars, lids, and screw rings (refer to page 29 for detailed instructions). Fill a canner or large stockpot with water, and set it over medium-high heat. Bring just to the boiling point. Place the lids in a small saucepan, fill with water, bring to a boil, turn off the heat, and set the pan aside.

4. Place the hot jars on top of a kitchen cloth on the counter. With the help of a canning funnel, pack chutney into the jars, reserving 1/2-inch (1.3 cm) headspace. Use a nonmetallic spatula to remove any trapped air bubbles, and wipe the rims clean with a damp cloth. Place on the lids and screw bands, tightening only until fingertip-tight.

5. Using a jar lifter, place the jars in the canner. Process 15 minutes in a boiling water bath (refer to page 32 for detailed instructions). Remember to adjust for altitude. **Variation:** To make peach chutney, simply replace the nectarines with an equal amount of peaches.

Peach and Lavender Butter

Whether found in wooden crates at farm stands, hanging from fruit-heavy branches, or with juices running steadily down chins, peaches are one of the stars of summer. Paired here with lavender and puréed to a velvety texture, this buttery spread will elevate biscuits, toast, and taste buds.

Yield: 6 half-pints

- 3 pounds peaches
- 1/3 cup water
- 2 tablespoons fresh or dried lavender buds
- 3 tablespoons bottled lemon juice
- 1 1/2 tablespoons lemon zest
- 3 cups granulated sugar

TO PREPARE:

1. Blanch the peaches following the instructions on page 52. Once the fruit is cool enough to handle, peel, pit, and chop roughly.

2. Bring 1/3 cup water to a boil. Place the lavender buds in a small bowl. Pour in the boiling water, cover, and steep for 15 minutes. Strain the liquid through a mesh sieve and set aside.

3. Sterilize 6 half-pint mason jars, lids, and screw rings (refer to page 29 for detailed instructions). Fill a canner or large stockpot with water, and set over medium-high heat. Bring just to the boiling point. Place the lids in a small saucepan, fill with water, bring to a boil, turn off the heat, and set the pan aside.

4. Combine the lavender water, peaches, lemon juice, and zest in a heavy, medium stainless-steel saucepan. Bring to a boil over medium-high heat. Reduce the heat and simmer for 15 minutes, until the peach mixture thickens and clings to a spoon. Remove from the heat.

5. Once the peach mixture has cooled slightly, either press it through a food mill or fine-meshed sieve or purée using a food processor or immersion blender.

6. Return the purée to the pan, add the sugar and lavender buds, and bring the mixture to a gentle boil over medium heat. Stir continually until the sugar is completely dissolved. Reduce the heat and simmer uncovered for 25 minutes.

7. Place the hot jars on top of a kitchen cloth on the counter. With the help of a canning funnel, pack peach butter into the jars, reserving 1/2-inch (1.3 cm) headspace. Use a nonmetallic spatula to remove any trapped air bubbles, and wipe the rims clean with a damp cloth. Place on the lids and screw bands, tightening only until fingertip-tight.

8. Using a jar lifter, place the jars in the canner. Process 10 minutes in a boiling water bath (refer to page 32 for detailed instructions). Remember to adjust for altitude.

Variation: Substitute an equal amount of peeled nectarines for the peaches. To introduce an additional layer of flavor, add 1/2 teaspoon ground allspice, 1/2 teaspoon ground cloves, and 1 teaspoon ground cinnamon.

Cherry and Lemon Thyme Marmalade

This marmalade truly captures summer in a bottle. Enjoy some during cooler months for a reminder of the pleasures of cherry season. Perfectly at home with toast and scones, this marmalade would also be delicious served up with pork tenderloin. While lemon thyme is ideal in this recipe, if it is unavailable, substitute an equal amount of regular thyme. *Yield: 6 half-pints*

YOU WILL NEED:

2 oranges

6 cups pitted sweet cherries

6 tablespoons bottled lemon juice

4³/4 cups granulated sugar

1 tablespoon fresh lemon thyme
    (1¹/2 teaspoons dried)

TO PREPARE:

1. Place two small plates in the freezer (these will be u later to test for gelling).

2. Sterilize 6 half-pint mason jars, lids, and screw ring (refer to page 29 for detailed instructions). Fill a canner large stockpot with water, and set over medium-high h Bring just to the boiling point. Place the lids in a small saucepan, fill with water, bring to a boil, turn off the he and set the pan aside.

3. Cut the oranges into quarters, and remove any seeds Leaving the peel on, chop the oranges into small pieces. the chopped oranges, cherries, and lemon juice into a lar heavy, stainless-steel saucepan. Bring the fruit mixture t boil, reduce heat, and simmer for 15 minutes. Add the su and lemon thyme, bring the heat back up to medium-hig and boil for 25 minutes, stirring frequently to prevent sti

4. Test for gelling. Remove a plate from the freezer, an spoon about 1 teaspoon of the marmalade onto it. Plac the plate back in the freezer and wait 2 minutes. Remo from the freezer, and push the edge of the marmalade with your fingertip. If it has gelled properly, the surface wrinkle a bit. If it fails to wrinkle, or is obviously still ru continue cooking the marmalade for 5 minutes longer, then repeat the test.

5. Place the hot jars on top of a kitchen cloth on the co With the help of a canning funnel, pack marmalade into jars, reserving ¹/4-inch (6 mm) headspace. Use a nonmet. spatula to remove any trapped air bubbles, and wipe the clean with a damp cloth. Place on the lids and screw bar tightening only until fingertip-tight.

6. Using a jar lifter, place the jars in the canner. Proce 15 minutes in a boiling water bath (refer to page 32 for detailed instructions). Remember to adjust for altitude.

Variation: For a more traditional marmalade, omit the lemon thyme altogether, or replace it with 2 teaspoons freshly grated ginger or 1¹/2 teaspoons ground ginger.

Pickled Okra

Okra is ideal for pickling. Once bathed in an herbaceous brine, the vegetable becomes succulent and luscious, perfect for enjoying on hot summer nights. Combine these pickles with a glass of iced tea or some white wine, and you've got the makings of a scrumptious summertime snack. Best made with pods no longer than 4 inches (10.2 cm) long, pickled okra would also make a fine garnish to a juicy tomato sandwich. *Yield: 4 pints*

YOU WILL NEED:

- 4 pounds okra
- 2 1/2 cups white vinegar
- 2 1/2 cups water
- 1/4 cup pickling or kosher salt
- 1/2 cup dill seed
- 4 cloves garlic, peeled
- 2 teaspoons crushed red pepper flakes

TO PREPARE:

1. Sterilize 4 pint-sized mason jars, lids, and screw rings (refer to page 29 for detailed instructions). Fill a canner or large stockpot with water, and set over medium-high heat. Bring just to the boiling point. Place the lids in a small saucepan, fill with water, bring to a boil, turn off the heat, and set the pan aside.

2. Wash the okra and trim ends, taking care not to pierce the pods. Set aside.

3. In a medium stainless-steel saucepan, combine the vinegar, water, and salt. Bring the pickling brine just to the boiling point, cover, and remove from the heat.

4. Place the hot jars on top of a kitchen cloth on the counter. Into each jar, place 2 tablespoons dill seed, 1 garlic clove, and 1/2 teaspoon crushed red pepper flakes.

5. Pack the okra points down into the jars; fill the jars snugly, but not too tightly. With the help of a canning funnel, ladle pickling brine over the okra, reserving 1/2-inch (1.3 cm) headspace. Use a nonmetallic spatula to remove any trapped air bubbles, and wipe the rims clean with a damp cloth. Place on the lids and screw bands, tightening only until fingertip-tight.

6. Using a jar lifter, place the jars in the canner. Process 10 minutes in a boiling water bath (refer to page 32 for detailed instructions). Remember to adjust for altitude. **Variation:** Replace the okra with an equal amount of green beans. Trim ends in the same manner, and follow directions as written.

Tomato Basil Sauce

When the mercury rises, tomatoes are the order of the day. Basil was practically made for tomatoes, and this flavor duet will entice diners to gather round the table no matter the season. Keep this sauce on hand to pour over pasta on nights when you don't feel like thinking too hard about what to serve for dinner.

Yield: 5 pints

YOU WILL NEED:

- 8 pounds tomatoes
- 2 cups onion, chopped
- 2 garlic cloves, minced
- 2 teaspoons granulated sugar
- 1½ teaspoons pickling or kosher salt
- ½ teaspoon ground black pepper
- ⅓ cup fresh basil, chopped
- 3 tablespoons balsamic vinegar
- 5 tablespoons bottled lemon juice

TO PREPARE:

1. Peel, core, and chop the tomatoes (see "Blanching" on page 52 for detailed instructions on removing peels). Place the tomatoes in a large, heavy, stainless-steel saucepan. Use a potato masher to crush the tomatoes, allowing their juices to be released. Bring to a boil over medium-high heat. Add the onion, garlic, sugar, salt, black pepper, and basil, and stir. Reduce the heat to medium and simmer for 1½ hours, stirring frequently to keep from sticking.

2. While the sauce cooks, sterilize 5 pint-sized mason jars, lids, and screw rings (refer to page 29 for detailed instructions). Fill a canner or large stockpot with water, and set over medium-high heat. Bring just to the boiling point. Place the lids in a small saucepan, fill with water, bring to a boil, turn off the heat, and set the pan aside.

3. Remove the sauce from the heat. Run the mixture through a food mill or fine sieve to remove any seeds. Discard the seeds, return the sauce to the saucepan, and bring back to a boil over medium-high heat. Cook for 5 minutes, then remove from heat. Stir in vinegar.

4. Place the hot jars on top of a kitchen cloth on the counter. Add 1 tablespoon lemon juice to the bottom of each jar. With the help of a canning funnel, ladle sauce into the jars, reserving ½-inch (1.3 cm) headspace. Use a nonmetallic spatula to remove any trapped air bubbles, and wipe the rims clean with a damp cloth. Place on the lids and screw bands, tightening only until fingertip-tight.

5. Using a jar lifter, place the jars in the canner. Process 35 minutes in a boiling water bath (refer to page 32 for detailed instructions). Remember to adjust for altitude.

Variation: Substitute 1 tablespoon each fresh oregano and fresh marjoram for the basil.

🍁 Autumn

It's easy to fall in love with autumn. The days are cooler and the trees pull out all the stops in a wild symphony of colors. Autumn also showcases some phenomenal fruits, including apples, pears, figs, and cranberries. Many vegetables of the season, such as beets, become sweeter with the drop in temperature. The kitchen is also now cooler for canning, making one last rush of preserving that much more pleasurable. Crack open a hard cider or steep a spicy mug of tea, and preserve the last of the year's harvest before bidding it a fond farewell.

Cranberry, Juniper, and Rosemary Sauce

Cranberries are autumn's ephemeral delight. Enjoy them fresh when you see them because they're guaranteed not to hang around for too long. Juniper is added in this recipe for its characteristic pine and citrus flavors. This sauce is a winner with turkey in any form as well as a perfect foil for sweet potatoes. **Yield: 3 pints or 6 half-pints**

YOU WILL NEED:

6 cups cranberries

3 cups granulated sugar

3 cups water

¼ cup juniper berries, lightly crushed*

2 tablespoons fresh rosemary, finely chopped

Zest and juice of 1 lime

*Available at natural food stores

TO PREPARE:

1. Sterilize 3 pint or 6 half-pint mason jars, lids, and screw rings (refer to page 29 for detailed instructions). Fill a canner or large stockpot with water, and set over medium-high heat. Bring just to the boiling point. Place the lids in a small saucepan, fill with water, bring to a boil, turn off the heat, and set the pan aside.

2. Rinse the cranberries under cool water. Set aside. In a large, heavy, stainless-steel saucepan, combine the sugar and 3 cups water. Bring to a boil over medium-high heat, reduce heat to medium, and boil until the sugar is completely dissolved, about 5 minutes. Add the cranberries and juniper berries. Simmer for 12 minutes, until the cranberries have burst, stirring occasionally to keep from sticking. Add the rosemary, lime juice, and zest, and cook an additional 5 minutes. Remove from the heat.

3. Place the hot jars on top of a kitchen cloth on the counter. With the help of a canning funnel, pack cranberry sauce into the jars, reserving ¼-inch (6 mm) headspace.

Use a nonmetallic spatula to remove any trapped air bubbles, and wipe the rims clean with a damp cloth. Place on the lids and screw bands, tightening only until fingertip-tight.

4. Using a jar lifter, place the jars in the canner. Process 15 minutes in a boiling water bath (refer to page 32 for detailed instructions). Remember to adjust for altitude.
Variation: Omit the rosemary and juniper berries, replacing with 2 tablespoons grated fresh ginger and 2 tablespoons orange zest.

Spiced Pear Chutney

Serve this homage to autumn with a block of sharp cheddar cheese, some cornichons, and hard cider. Alternatively, slather it on a ham sandwich for a winning sweet-salty-sour trifecta! *Yield: 6 half-pints*

YOU WILL NEED:

4	pounds pears, peeled, cored, and diced
1	yellow onion, chopped
1 ½	cups seedless raisins
1	cup golden raisins
2	cloves garlic, minced
3	cups dark brown sugar
3	cups cider vinegar
½	cup water
2	tablespoons crystallized ginger, minced
2	teaspoons ground cinnamon
½	teaspoon ground cloves
½	teaspoon ground nutmeg
1	tablespoon yellow mustard seed
1 ½	teaspoons salt

TO PREPARE:

1. Place all the ingredients in a large, heavy, stainless steel saucepan. Bring to a boil over medium-high heat. Reduce the heat and simmer uncovered for around 1½ hours, or until the volume is reduced by half, stirring occasionally to prevent sticking.

2. While the chutney cooks, sterilize 6 half-pint mason jars, lids, and screw rings (refer to page 29 for detailed instructions). Fill a canner large stockpot with water and set over medium-high heat. Bring just to the boiling point. Place the lids in a small saucepan, fill with water, bring to a boil, turn off the heat, and set the pan aside.

3. Place the hot jars on top of a kitchen cloth on the counter. Pack chutney into the jars, reserving ¼ inch (6 mm) headspace. Use a nonmetallic spatula to remove any trapped air bubbles and wipe the rims clean with a damp cloth. Place on the lids and screw bands, tightening only until fingertip-tight.

4. Using a jar lifter, place the jars in the canner. Process 10 minutes in a boiling water bath (refer to page 32 for detailed instructions). Remember to adjust for altitude.
Variation: For a spicy apple chutney, replace the pears with an equal amount of apples.

Cardamom Apple Cider Butter

Cardamom offers an unexpected twist on a seasonal favorite. Prepare apple butter in season, when apples are at their peak of ripeness, to best capture the fruit at its finest. Cooking apples such as Golden Delicious, Granny Smith, Gravenstein, McIntosh, Newton, Pippin, or Winesap, will shine in this recipe. *Yield: 6 half-pints*

5 pounds cooking apples, peeled, cored, and coarsely chopped

1½ cups apple cider

2½ cups granulated sugar

1 tablespoon ground cardamom*

*For a more intense cardamom flavor, remove the seeds from 4 cardamom pods and grind them until powdered in a coffee grinder or spice mill.

TO PREPARE:

1. Place the apples and cider in a large stainless-steel pot. Bring to a boil over medium-high heat. Reduce the heat and simmer for 25 minutes, stirring occasionally to prevent sticking. If additional liquid is necessary, add water in tablespoon increments. Remove from the heat.

2. Once the cooked apple mixture is slightly cooled, purée it using a food processor or immersion blender or by pressing through a food mill or fine-meshed sieve. Blend the apples just until smooth but not runny.

3. Return the purée to the pot, add the sugar and cardamom, and bring the mixture to a gentle boil over medium heat. Reduce the heat to low and simmer for 25 to 30 minutes until the apple butter thickens and clings to a spoon. Stir often to prevent the mixture from sticking. Remove from the heat.

4. While the apple butter cooks, sterilize 6 half-pint mason jars, lids, and screw rings (refer to page 29 for detailed instructions). Fill a canner or large stockpot with water, and set over medium-high heat. Bring just to the boiling point. Place the lids in a small saucepan, fill with water, bring to a boil, turn off the heat, and set the pan aside.

5. Place the hot jars on top of a kitchen cloth on the counter. With the help of a canning funnel, pack apple butter into the jars, reserving ¼-inch (6 mm) headspace. Use a nonmetallic spatula to remove any trapped air bubbles, and wipe the rims clean with a damp cloth. Place on the lids and screw bands, tightening only until fingertip-tight.

6. Using a jar lifter, place the jars in the canner. Process 10 minutes in a boiling water bath (refer to page 32 for detailed instructions). Remember to adjust for altitude.
Variation: For a "tipsy" butter, reduce sugar by ½ cup. About 15 minutes into the cooking time, add ½ cup brandy, and continue as written.

Fig and Thyme Jam

Autumn offers an abundance of plump, moist, and delicious fresh figs. Thyme adds an element of flavor sophistication to this jam, which would be heavenly atop a wheel of brie, swaddled in phyllo pastry, and baked to golden perfection.

Yield: 6 half-pints

YOU WILL NEED:

4	pounds fresh figs
1	tablespoon dry pectin
4 1/2	cups granulated sugar
1/4	cup bottled lemon juice
1/2	cup water
2	teaspoons fresh thyme (1 teaspoon dried)

TO PREPARE:

1. Place two small plates in the freezer (these will be used later to test for gelling).

2. Sterilize 6 half-pint mason jars, lids, and screw ri (refer to page 29 for detailed instructions). Fill a cann or large stockpot with water, and set over medium-h heat. Bring just to the boiling point. Place lids in a sm saucepan, fill with water, bring to a boil, turn off hea remove from stovetop, and set the pan aside.

3. Wash the figs and gently pat them dry. Trim their stems and bottoms, and then chop into medium piec Empty the pectin packet into a small bowl, add 1/4 cu sugar, and stir to incorporate.

4. In a large, heavy, stainless-steel saucepan, combi the figs, pectin-sugar mixture, lemon juice, and wate Bring to a boil over medium-high heat, stirring const until sugar is dissolved. Add the remaining sugar and thyme; stir until sugar is completely dissolved. Resum boiling and cook 4 additional minutes. Use a slotted or skimmer to remove any foam that forms on the to the jam as it cooks.

5. Test for gelling. Remove a plate from the freezer a spoon about 1 teaspoon of the jam onto it. Place the back in the freezer, and wait 2 minutes. Remove from freezer and push the edge of the jam with your finge If it has gelled properly, the surface will wrinkle a bit fails to wrinkle, or is obviously still runny, continue c ing the jam for 5 minutes longer, and then repeat the

6. Once you are sure the jam has set, remove the sa pan from heat and allow it to sit, covered, for 5 minu This short rest will help keep pieces of fig from separ from the juice once the jam is jarred.

7. Place the hot jars on top of a kitchen cloth on the counter. With the help of a canning funnel, pack jam the jars, reserving 1/4-inch (6 mm) headspace. Use a n metallic spatula to remove any trapped air bubbles, a wipe the rims clean with a damp cloth. Place on the and screw bands, tightening only until fingertip-tight

8. Using a jar lifter, place the jars in the canner. Proc 10 minutes in a boiling water bath (refer to page 32 fo detailed instructions). Remember to adjust for altitud

Variation: For a more traditional fig jam, omit the thy Alternatively, replace the thyme with 1 teaspoon of ground cinnamon.

Beet and Sage Relish

Come autumn, farmers' markets offer a bounty of beets in a rainbow of colors, from the most resplendent gold to the darkest burgundy. Redolent of soil and nectar, beets offer something for everyone. Try this relish on a hummus sandwich, or dollop a small amount on top of deviled eggs. *Yield: 4 pints*

YOU WILL NEED:

- 5 medium beets
- 3 cups red cabbage, finely shredded
- 2 tablespoons fresh horseradish root, or 1 tablespoon prepared horseradish
- 2 ¾ cup cider vinegar
- 1 cup granulated sugar
- 1 tablespoon fresh sage, chopped (1½ teaspoons dried)
- 2 ½ teaspoons pickling or kosher salt

TO PREPARE:

1. Blanch the beets following the instructions on page 52. Once they are cool enough to handle, peel and chop roughly.

2. Sterilize 4 pint-sized mason jars, lids, and screw rings (refer to page 29 for detailed instructions). Fill canner or large stockpot with water, and set over medium-high heat. Bring just to the boiling point. Place the lids in a small saucepan, fill with water, bring to a boil, turn off the heat, and set the pan aside.

3. Combine all ingredients in a large, heavy, stainless-steel saucepan. Bring to a boil over medium-high heat, reduce to low, and simmer for 20 minutes. Remove from heat.

4. Place the hot jars on top of a kitchen cloth on the counter. With the help of a canning funnel, pack relish into the jars, reserving ½-inch (1.3 cm) headspace. Use a nonmetallic spatula to remove any trapped air bubbles, and wipe the rims clean with a damp cloth. Place on the lids and screw bands, tightening only until fingertip-tight.

5. Using a jar lifter, place the jars in the canner. Process 15 minutes in a boiling water bath (refer to page 32 for detailed instructions). Remember to adjust for altitude.
Variation: Replace the sage with an equal amount of fresh rosemary.

Resources

With the tables below you can make the recipes in this book using metric measuring instruments. All conversions are approximate.

Metric Conversion Chart by Volume (for Liquids)

U.S.	Metric (milliliters/liters)
1/4 teaspoon	1.25 mL
1/2 teaspoon	2.5 mL
1 teaspoon	5 mL
1 tablespoon	15 mL
1/4 cup	60 mL
1/2 cup	120 mL
3/4 cup	180 mL
1 cup	240 mL
2 cups (1 pint)	480 mL
4 cups (1 quart)	960 mL
4 quarts (1 gallon)	3.8 L

Metric Conversion Chart by Weight (for Dry Ingredients)

U.S.	Metric (grams/kilograms)
1/4 teaspoon	1 g
1/2 teaspoon	2 g
1 teaspoon	5 g
1 tablespoon	15 g
16 ounces (1 pound)	450 g
2 pounds	900 g
3 pounds	1.4 kg
4 pounds	1.8 kg
5 pounds	2.3 kg
6 pounds	2.7 kg

Cooking Measurement Equivalents

3 teaspoons = 1 tablespoon

2 tablespoons = 1 fluid ounce

4 tablespoons = 1/4 cup

5 tablespoons + 1 teaspoon = 1/3 cup

8 tablespoons = 1/2 cup

10 tablespoons + 2 teaspoons = 2/3 cup

12 tablespoons = 3/4 cup

16 tablespoons = 1 cup

48 teaspoons = 1 cup

1 cup = 8 fluid ounces

2 cups = 1 pint

2 pints = 1 quart

4 quarts = 1 gallon

Altitude Adjustment Chart

Altitude Variations for Boiling Water Bath Processing

Altitude in Feet (Meters)	Processing Time
0–1000 (0–300 m)	Time in recipe
1001–3000 (301–900 m)	Add 5 minutes
3001–6000 (901–1800 m)	Add 10 minutes
6001–8000 (1801–2400 m)	Add 15 minutes
8001–10000 (2401–3000 m)	Add 20 minutes

Altitude Variations for Pressure Canning Processing

Altitude in Feet (Meters)	Weighted Gauge	Dial Gauge
0–1000 (0–301 m)	10	11
1001–2000 (301–600 m)	15	11
2001–4000 (601–1200 m)	15	12
4001–6000 (1201–1800 m)	15	13
6001–8000 (1801–2400 m)	15	14
8001–10000 (2401–3000 m)	15	15

MAIL-ORDER SUPPLIERS

Jars, Lids, Water-Bath Canners, Pressure Canners, Food Mills, Strainers, and Tools

Canning Pantry
800-285-9044
www.canningpantry.com

Canning USA
www.canningusa.com

Jarden Home Brands/Bernardin Ltd.
800-240-3340
www.freshpreserving.com or
www.homecanning.com/can (Canada)

Kitchen Krafts
800-298-5389
www.kitchenkrafts.com

Lehman's
877-438-5346
www.lehmans.com

Leifheit Jars available at Sur la Table
www.surlatable.com

Spices and Herbs

Frontier
www.frontiercoop.com

Penzeys
www.penzeys.com

Simply Organic
www.simplyorganicfoods.com

Vinegar

Bragg Health Products
www.bragg.com

Eden Organic
www.edenfoods.com

Spectrum
www.spectrumorganics.com

Sugar

Florida Crystals
www.floridacrystals.com

Wholesome Sweeteners
www.wholesomesweeteners.com

Pectin

Pomona's Universal Pectin
www.pomonapectin.com

Pickling and Kosher Salt

Morton Canning and Pickling Salt
www.mortonsalt.com

Mrs. Wages Canning and Pickling Salt
www.mrswages.com

FARMERS' MARKETS AND U-PICK

Local Harvest
A comprehensive U.S. listing of farmers' markets
www.localharvest.org

Pick Your Own
U.S. and international listings of U-pick farms
www.pickyourown.org

PERIODICALS

The following publications often contain useful information on home preserving:

BackHome
www.backhomemagazine.com

Grit
www.grit.com

Hobby Farms Home
www.hobbyfarms.com

Mother Earth News
www.motherearthnews.com

A NOTE FROM THE AUTHOR: It takes a good bit of time for a book to make its way from initial idea to printed copy. That means that as helpful as a list like this one is, by the time you're holding your book in your hands, it's inevitable that some of the websites or physical addresses will have changed and that useful new resources will have surfaced. Still, it's a great starting point for those just entering the world of all things canning. And about those changes and updates? I'm tracking them all in a regularly updated Resources section of my blog. Be sure to visit me regularly there: www.small-measure.blogspot.com.

Notes

MARKET FRESH

Freshness counts. I can't emphasize it enough. Just-picked fruits and vegetables are at their peak in terms of flavor, texture, and nutrition. For some items, such as cucumbers and corn, home canning is successful only if the items are put up right after harvest, as intrinsic enzymes can compromise their ability to maintain quality once jarred. That is why shopping, growing, and canning of fruits and vegetables are best done when they are in season. The following lists offer a season-by-season guide to what is available to the home canner. Keep these seasonal offerings in mind when you head out to the market or start eyeballing seed catalogues. Be advised that these listings may differ for those not living in North America.

Winter

- Brussels sprouts
- Celeriac
- Citrus fruits
- Fennel
- Kale
- Leeks
- Parsnips
- Rutabagas
- Turnips

Spring

- Apricots
- Artichokes
- Asparagus
- Broccoli
- Celery
- Peas
- New potatoes
- Radishes
- Ramps
- Rhubarb
- Scallions
- Spinach
- Strawberries

Summer

- Blackberries
- Blueberries
- Cherries
- Corn
- Cucumbers
- Currants
- Eggplant
- Garlic
- Green beans
- Melons
- Nectarines
- Okra
- Onions
- Peaches
- Peppers
- Plums
- Raspberries
- Tomatoes
- Yellow squash
- Zucchini

Autumn

- Apples
- Beets
- Cabbage
- Cauliflower
- Collard greens
- Cranberries
- Figs
- Grapes
- Mushrooms
- Pears
- Pomegranates
- Potatoes
- Pumpkin
- Sweet potatoes
- Swiss chard
- Winter squash

AS THE CANNER BOILS

Sometimes it's nice to look back over the years at all you've managed to put up. While your pantry shelves will reveal more recent contributions, keeping notes affords you the opportunity to reflect back on the last time you canned peaches, say, or made fig jam. Use this journal to chronicle your efforts and to provide some backup in the event that you should overlook dating your jars.

Year: _____
Canned: _____
_____
_____
_____
_____
_____
_____
_____
_____
_____

Year: _____
Canned: _____
_____
_____
_____
_____
_____
_____
_____
_____
_____

Year: _____
Canned: _____
_____
_____
_____
_____
_____
_____
_____

Year: _____
Canned: _____
_____
_____
_____
_____
_____
_____
_____

Glossary

Acidify. The process of using vinegar or other sour ingredients to raise the level of acid in foods; this allows foods with an otherwise low acid level to be safely processed in a boiling water bath.

Altitude Adjustment. The process of modifying processing times to account for variations in altitude; standard processing amounts are based on conditions at sea level or up to 1000 feet (300 m) in elevation. As elevation increases, water boils at increasingly lower temperatures. In order to ensure that harmful bacteria are killed, processing times must be increased.

Ascorbic Acid. More commonly known as Vitamin C, a water-soluble vitamin available in tablet or powdered form; ascorbic acid is used in canning to prevent discoloration of certain fruits during preparation.

Blanch. To drop fruits or vegetables into rapidly boiling water for a very brief time; this is done to deactivate enzymatic actions that would otherwise cause browning. Blanching also loosens peels, making them easier to remove. Blanched produce items are submerged into an ice water bath immediately after boiling.

Boiling Water Bath. One of the two processing methods for home canning; a boiling water bath can be used to preserve high-acid foods, including foods that have been acidified. In this method, water is brought to a boil in a large kettle or stockpot, filled mason jars with two-piece closures are submerged, and the jars are left to boil for a specific period of time. This processing method destroys yeasts, some types of bacteria, and mold, in addition to deactivating enzymes.

Botulism. An odorless, colorless, and potentially lethal type of food poisoning caused by the spores of *Clostridium botulinum*; they are found primarily on low-acid foods, which must be processed in a pressure canner, as this is the only way to ensure they have been destroyed. Killing botulism spores requires a higher temperature than that which can be achieved in a boiling water bath.

Brine. A solution of salt and water used in making pickles; sugar and herbs are sometimes added as well.

Canner. One of two pieces of equipment used in home canning; for boiling water bath processing, a kettle or large stockpot is used. For pressure canning, either a dial-gauge or weighted-gauge pressure canner is used.

Cheesecloth. A fine, thin woven cloth used in a number of cooking techniques; in home canning, cheesecloth can be used for straining jelly or as a pouch for holding herbs and spices during cooking.

Dial-gauge Pressure Canner. A type pressure canner equipped with a pressure regulator and a gauge that gives exact numeric readings of the pressure inside the canner; if the pressure is too low or too high, raising or lowering the heat level of the burner adjusts it. Dial-gauge pressure canners must be checked annually for accuracy.

Exhausting. Also known as "venting," this is a necessary step in pressure canning that forces all the air inside the canner out. Air is allowed to escape from the vent on the lid of a pressure canner for no less than 10 minutes. Failure to vent adequately could alter temperatures inside the canner and result in improperly sealed food. Exhausting must be done every time a pressure canner is used.

Fingertip-tight. This is the tension that should be applied to screw bands when attaching them to jars. Tighten the screw band until resistance is met, then apply slightly more pressure until the band is attached only as firmly as your fingertips could easily remove it.

Food Mill. A hand-cranked sieve used in cooking to purée foods; the seeds and skins of foods are collected in the top part of the sieve, while the purée accumulates in the bottom half.

Gel Stage. The point reached in the production of jams, jellies, marmalades, and butters where soft spreads gel and hold their shape; this occurs when the pectin in the mixture solidifies, usually around 220°F (104°C).

Headspace. This is the space between the top of the food in the jar and the underside of the lid. Generally, whole fruits and any pickled and acidified foods such as chutneys, relishes, pickles, condiments, and tomatoes require 1/2-inch (1.3 cm) headspace, while fruit spreads and juices need 1/4-inch (6 mm) headspace. Providing accurate headspace is vital to creating a proper seal, as well as for keeping a jar's contents inside where they belong.

High-acid Food. Refers to foods that have enough acid, either naturally or as an added ingredient, to achieve a pH level of 4.6 or lower; many fruits are naturally high-acid; fruit juices, jams, jellies, tomatoes, and other types of soft spreads are normally high-acid as well. Most vegetables are low-acid and can only become high-acid through the addition of an acidifying agent such as vinegar or lemon juice.

Hot Pack. A canning method that involves cooking ingredients before placing them into jars; the hot pack method forces trapped air out of fruit or vegetable tissues before they are jarred, helping to form a tighter vacuum seal. It also prevents items from floating.

Lid. One part of the two-piece closures used for topping jars in home canning; the flat lids are fashioned from tin-plated steel that has been covered in a food-grade coating. Running the circumference of the underside of the lid is a rubber compound, specially formulated for vacuum-sealing foods canned at home. Lids should be used only once.

Low-acid Food. Foods that are low in naturally occurring acid; vegetables, meats, seafood, and dairy products are low-acid and must be processed in a pressure canner in order to be safe for use in home canning. If low-acid foods are made more acidic through an acidifying agent, they can be safely canned using the boiling water bath method.

Mason Jar. A generic term now used to describe the model of jar developed by John Mason during the mid-19th century; the jars are made of tempered glass that is safe for use in either a boiling water bath or a pressure canner. Two-piece lids, which screw on to threaded rings at the neck, create a vacuum seal during processing. The jars are available in regular or wide-mouth varieties and range in size from 4 ounces to 1 gallon (120 mL to 3.8 L). So long as they remain crack free, mason jars may be reused indefinitely.

Pectin. A naturally occurring, water-soluble type of carbohydrate that is found in the tissue, skin, and seeds of all fruits; pectin reacts with sugar and acid to create a gel, or bond. Depending on whether the fruit you are using is naturally high or low in pectin, the addition of commercially prepared pectin may be necessary to achieve a gel.

pH. Literally the "potential of hydrogen," this measuring system is used by chemists to determine a solution's acidity or alkalinity. High pH values are low-acid, while low pH values indicate high acidity. In home canning, a food's pH value determines whether it needs to be processed in a boiling water bath or a pressure canner. Foods with a pH of 4.6 or lower are generally considered safe to can using the boiling water bath method.

Pickling. This is a form of food preservation in which fruits or vegetables are submerged in a high-acid solution, such as brine or vinegar, and allowed to cure, or develop flavor, over time. Often herbs and spices are added, as well as sugar.

Glossary (continued)

Pickling Salt. Salt specifically indicated for home-canning use; listed in stores as either "pickling" or "kosher," these salts are free of iodine and anticaking additives and are very fine-grained, allowing them to dissolve easily.

Pressure Canner. A tall metal pot equipped with a locking lid containing a pressure-regulating gauge; this type of canner creates steam inside the pot, allowing temperatures of 240 to 250°F (115 to 121°C) to be reached. If you intend to can any low-acid foods, then a pressure canner is absolutely essential.

Process. The term used to describe the act of preserving foods in a boiling water bath or pressure canner; heated jars are filled with foods and subjected to high temperatures for specific periods of time in order to kill off harmful molds, yeasts, bacteria, and enzymes. Processing allows foods to be safely preserved at home.

Raw Pack. Sometimes referred to as the "cold pack" method, raw pack involves packing jars with raw, uncooked ingredients, and then processing them. While this method is certainly faster than heat packing, it often results in foods shrinking and floating once jarred.

Screw Band. One part of the two-piece closures used for topping jars in home canning; these threaded metal bands fit atop the lids, securing them in place over the neck of the glass jar. During processing, the screw bands hold down the lids, allowing the sealing compound to secure the lid to the jar.

Shelf Life. The length of time a processed food remains good to eat; foods are their freshest and most tasty when consumed within their shelf life. In home canning, foods should ideally be eaten within one year of preparation.

Spice Bag. A fabric pouch fashioned out of either cheesecloth or muslin into which whole spices and herbs are placed; the spice bag is then placed in with the ingredients during cooking and removed before the jars are filled. Using a spice bag allows flavors to be imparted into a product without the added risk of discoloration or too strong a taste that might occur should the spices remain in the mixture once jarred.

Sterlize. The process of killing any living organisms; in home canning, this is achieved before processing by submerging jars in boiling water for 10 minutes as well as during processing itself by placing filled jars into either a boiling water bath or a pressure canner for a specified length of time.

Vacuum Seal. The absence of normal air pressure and atmospheric conditions that happens when filled jars are heat processed; as the jars' contents are heated, they expand, forcing air out. Once cooled, the contents shrink, creating a vacuum. The rubber compound surrounding the underside of canning lids reinforces this vacuum and aids in preventing air from getting back into the jar. Vacuum sealing prevents spoilage and keeps harmful pathogens out of preserved foods.

Weighted-gauge Pressure Canner. A type of pressure canner that is fitted with a weighted pressure adjustment; these models allow small quantities of steam to escape from the lid every time the gauge whistles or rocks back and forth during processing. Altitude adjustments must be made on weighted-gauge pressure canners, as their accuracy is affected by changes in elevation.

Acknowledgments

An overflowing garden of gratitude is in order for the many talented individuals who pulled together this project.

To the wonderful profilees: Jenny Bartoy, Chris Bryant, Amy Deaver, Harriet Fasenfest, Walter Harrill, Rachel Saunders, Donna Sharpe, Libby Woodruff, and Lisa Wujnovich. Thank you all for putting a smiling, jam-stained, pickle-puckered face to the many different ways we can all enjoy the benefits of canning and preserving in our lives.

I applaud Rebecca Springer for waving her copyediting wand over my words with grace and good judgment.

Photographer Lynne Harty never ceased to surprise with her ability to get just the right shot over and over again. Designer Eric Stevens should be lauded for his beautiful design, illustrations, and flawless ability to pull all of the puzzle pieces together in just the right way. Gratitude goes to Margaret Clough for her lovely winter photo. I'd also like to thank Devan Adams, Theo Adams, Meredith Law, and Nicole McConville for joining in on the canning party photo shoot.

Abundant gratitude is offered to Chris Bryant for letting us shine a spotlight on his own pickling prowess in one of the profiles, sharing his beautiful home for our photo shoot, offering invaluable canning knowledge, and providing an incredible penchant for knowing exactly how to capture the real beauty in food's riches.

Heartfelt thanks to Nicóle McConville, for believing I had both the skills and gumption to take on this book and the series. I am immeasurably grateful to have such a great friend and editor wrapped up in one convenient package.

For my long-suffering, infinitely patient husband, Glenn, who served as cheerleader, therapist, and official taster through all of this, I appreciate you more than you could ever know.

Finally, special thanks to Meaghan Finnerty, Paige Gilchrist, and Marcus Leaver for all of the excitement surrounding the series that you have both nurtured and enabled.

Also Available in the Homemade Living series:

AVAILABLE SPRING 2011:
Home Dairy *with Ashley English*
Keeping Bees *with Ashley English*

Photo Credits

The pages of this book are richer thanks to the contributed photos. Much gratitude is owed to the following individuals: Kevin Bartoy (page 36), Mark Bernfild (page 41), Chris Bryant (page 55), Shane Dunau (page 59), Ashley English (page 53), Brian Hershberger (page 87), Leah Nash (page 25), Donna Sharpe (page 59), Skip Wade (page 78), and Deborah Woodruff (page 15).

Index